Ra

Inspirational Articles

by

James Richards

Compiled and Edited by

Kaye Lynne Booth

Dan,

You're amazing! I really appreciate your faithfulness to Jesus. God bless.

Jim

Table of Contents

Raise the Tide
Inspirational Articles
by
James Richards

Introduction
Raise the Tide

THE COPALIS RIVER STARTS its course southwest of the majestic Olympic Mountains, meandering through the temperate coastal Rain Forest of Western Washington before it finally reaches its destination with the mighty Pacific Ocean. It's a small river, really not much more than a large creek for much of its journey, until it reaches the coastal lowlands, where it forms a wide five-mile long estuary.

Estuaries form where rivers reach the ocean and are impacted by the ocean's tides. Twice a day the ocean saltwater rushes up stream, filling the estuary at high tide, and twice a day it empties back into the ocean at low tide. The tide at the mouth of the Copalis River varies from -2 feet to +13 feet, so the river rises and falls as much as 15 feet twice daily, changing it considerably every 12 hours. The Copalis River estuary flourishes with life because saltwater mixes with fresh water, creating an ideal living situation for many species of plants, fish, birds and animals.

The lower portion of the estuary is bordered by native beachgrasses, which make a perfect home for many species of birds. Further upriver, one encounters the Copalis Ghost Forest, where giant dead Spruce trees punctuate the sky and give mute testimony to the power of the Tsunami that flooded the area in 1700. The upper reaches of the estuary are surrounded by thick forests of Douglas Fir, Hemlock, Cedar, and Alder trees. An older, decaying railroad trestle crosses the river there as a reminder of the bygone glory days of logging.

The river is full of life. Dungeness crabs mate in the lower section of the river in the summer; Silver Salmon swim upriver every fall to mate and their fingerling offspring return to the ocean the next summer, to repeat the cycle over and over; otters frolic on the banks of the river, feeding on many kinds of aquatic fish; Canadian geese land on the river every Spring and Fall as they rest on their marathon journey flying north or south; Lynx, Cougars, Black Bears and Coyotes hunt for mice, Cottontail Rabbits and Blacktail Deer that populate the area.

When the tide is low, the river is mostly mudflats and difficult to navigate. If you can catch the incoming tide, though, you fairly fly upriver in your canoe or kayak and can reach its remotest spots. It's exhilarating to feel the power of the tide as it charges upriver and carries you along with it, the river doing the majority of the work.

The Copalis River reminds me of the River of Life that flows from the throne of God. John saw "...the river of the water of life, as clear as crystal, flowing from the throne of God and of the Lamb down the middle of the great street of the city. On each side of the river stood the tree of life, bearing twelve crops of fruit every month" (Rev. 22:1,2). Ezekiel describes the same river, which gets deeper the farther you go. About this river he says," ...so where the river flows everything will live" (Ez. 47:9).

Where the river flows there is life! I believe the river is symbolical of the Holy Spirit. 2 Cor. 3:6 tells us "He has made us competent as ministers of a new covenant – not of the letter but of the Spirit: for the letter kills, but the Spirit gives life." Where the Holy Spirit moves there is life and power!

If we want to see God move in and through our lives, we need to allow the Spirit to raise the tide in our lives, which I believe happens when one "sows to please the Spirit" (Gal. 6:8). When I've done this, I can say with Paul "That my message and my preaching were not done with wise and persuasive words, but with a demonstration of the Spirit's power, so that your faith might not rest on men's wisdom, but on God's power." (1 Cor. 2:4). When the Spirit moves in our lives it's as if we are being carried along by a massive tide that does more than anyone could imagine or comprehend, which glorifies God.

I've written these weekly articles with the object of encouraging people to seek the Lord, believing that He still works in our lives, using us for His glory. My prayer is that these little articles will encourage you to grow in Christ, love Him more, and allow the Holy Spirit to use you for God's glory. Let the River flow!

Week 1
The Test

THE SMELL OF CEDAR was strong as I walked into the woods on my first job. As an axman on the survey crew I would help clear a line through the brush and woods of the Olympic National Forest so that the transit man could survey for building new logging roads. That first job brings many things for a green, raw recruit like me, not the least of which is the good-natured ribbing and practical jokes of the older men.

They laughed their heads off after I had returned from a mile walk to the van and had to ask, "What does a sky hook look like? I couldn't find it." They rolled on the ground in glee when one of the men asked to see my ax during a lunch break ax throwing contest and then abruptly stuck it twenty-five feet high in the target tree.

Their last laugh that summer was their best one, though. They had been priming me all summer to take the axmen's test. Finally, impatient to prove my ability, I volunteered to take the test. They agreed that I was ready. They whipped out a blindfold, chopped a notch in a log and placed me in the starting position.

Blindfolded, I had to hit the notch in the log ten times in a row with my ax to pass the test. I pulled the razor-sharp double-bitted ax up and chopped once, twice, three times! I knew I was in the grove and quickly chopped seven more times. Anxious to see my results, I yanked the blindfold off.

The guys had been hooting and hollering while I was chopping and the reason for their excitement stared me in the face. My ax had hit the mark okay, but, unfortunately, they had thrown my red sweatshirt on the log and it was chopped to ribbons. The axman's test, which I was so confident to take, wasn't a test after all, but a final joke on me. Passing their test was impossible once I fell for it. My face flushed redder than my chopped-up red sweatshirt when I realized I had been made a fool.

That reminds me of another test. All of us want to go to heaven someday and Satan convinces us that we must pass a test to get there. Like me and the axman's test, we are confident we can pass the test for eternal life. The test comes in many different forms – keeping the Ten Commandments for some, following church rules for others, living a good moral life for many, and just plain doing our best for most. We know we are not perfect, but we give it our best shot and feel confident that we will pass the test, whatever it is. After all, we think, there are lots of people who are doing worse than we are.

The only problem is that one day, at the end of our lives, the blindfold comes off and we see that it is an unfair test. The joke is on us because it is impossible to pass a test to get into heaven. The standard that is used to spend eternity with God is the life of Jesus Christ, and we fall terribly short of His perfection. The Bible says, *"All have sinned and fallen short of the glory of God" (Rom. 3:23); "without holiness no one will see the Lord" (Heb. 12:14);* and *"For whoever keeps the whole law and yet stumbles at just one point is guilty of breaking all of it." (James 2:10)*

Since it is impossible to pass a test to gain eternal life, what do we do? We refuse to take the test, admitting to ourselves that we can never meet the righteous requirements of God, and we put our trust in Jesus Christ, who took and passed the test for us. Jesus Christ came into the world as a human, lived a perfect, sinless life, and sacrificed Himself for our sins. He became the perfect sacrifice for our sins when He went to the cross and, now, He offers eternal life to all who put their trust in Him. When someone gives their life to Jesus Christ, His life is in them, and their life is in Him, and the Father accepts them based on the imputed righteousness of Jesus Christ in them. Romans 3:21, 22 tells us, *"But now a righteousness from God, apart from law, has been made known. This righteousness from God comes through faith in Jesus Christ to all who believe."*

When I took the axman's test, I lost a sweatshirt and my pride. When we stand before God and He asks us why we never put our trust in His Son Jesus, we stand to lose so much more - our souls for eternity. If you haven't done so yet, confess your sin to God and put your faith in Jesus Christ, asking Him to be your Savior, Lord and life. The Apostle Paul says, *"For the love of Christ controls us, because we have concluded this: that one has died for all, therefore all have died; and He died for all, that those who live might no longer live for themselves but for Him who for their sake died and was raised." (1 Cor. 5:14-15)*

Jesus took and passed the test for you – put your trust in Him!

Week 2
Blisters

"WHERE'S LESTER?" I asked his wife as I stood on her porch.

"He's fencing outback," she answered. "Just follow the fence line by the side of the house and you'll find him."

I hopped off the porch and followed the fence line to the back of their property. Lester was glad to see me, and after visiting a few minutes, I volunteered to help with his fencing project. He eagerly accepted my offer and told me my job would be pounding the fence posts into the ground so he could string the barb wire to keep his animals safe on his property.

He handed me a modified car driveline, which had been welded closed on one end, to pound the posts into the ground. I slipped the driveline over the first fence post, lifted it as high as I could, and slammed it down. The fence post sank a couple of inches into the ground and I repeated the process over and over until I heard the unmistakable sound of steel hitting rock. The fencepost refused to sink further into the ground.

I turned to Lester and commented, "This ground is rocky, isn't it?"

"Yeah," Lester casually answered, "you may have to move the post a foot or two either way to get it to go."

Oh, great, I thought. I get to pound each one of these posts two or three times! I started second guessing my offer to help.

All went well until the third post. That's when my hands started feeling hot. Obviously, my preacher hands were not in shape for this kind of work, especially without gloves. By the fifth post, several blisters popped out on each hand and I was painfully aware that I still had three more posts to go.

"I'm getting blisters," I hinted to Lester, hoping that he would relieve me and drive the remaining three posts.

He smiled at me and replied, "They'll heal." It was obvious I wasn't going to get any sympathy from Lester, so I kept pounding the posts in.

Well, Lester was right, my blisters eventually healed, even though my hands looked like hamburger by the time I finished all the posts. I only wish that, somehow, Lester could have shared the pain with me!

Blisters are God's alarm system. When they start forming, they warn us against damaging sensitive skin tissue. Without blisters we could easily hurt ourselves. Blisters also help cushion our skin from whatever is chafing it. Of course, as any workingman knows, if you keep working, the blisters eventually turn to hard callouses, allowing you to do the work without pain.

Our conscience is much like a blister. When we engage in sinful or harmful activities, our conscience sounds an alarm, warning us about activities that hurt us. Our conscience isn't intended to hurt us, but to warn us of activities that do. Just like a blister, though, our conscience becomes hardened and calloused if we continue that activity, until, eventually, we feel no pain. When this happens, we become insensitive to sin and it no longer bothers us. That's alright with blisters, but it is deadly when it comes to the conscience.

Even though our consciences aren't perfect, God has given one to all of us to help protect us from things that hurt us. If we ignore our conscience, we go further and further into sin until it hardens our heart, becoming a habitual life practice that eventually leads us to destruction.

Proverbs 4:23 warns us, *"Above all else, guard your heart, for it is the wellspring of life." (NIV)* Our heart, which includes the conscience, is the wellspring of our lives. If we guard our heart from sin, our heart remains pure and clean, working the way God intended it to work. If we don't guard our heart, though, the impurity of sin pollutes our lives, exposing us to more and more harmful activities that sicken the soul. Over time, the polluted heart produces destruction and death.

The next time your conscience sounds the alarm, pay attention to it. It is God's warning siren alerting you to dangers that produce hurt and destruction in your life. If your conscience has been hardened by sin, ask Jesus Christ to give you a new heart that is pure and clean. Jesus promises a new heart to all who put their trust in Him.

We can't afford to ignore our consciences – the results are too costly.

Week 3

Jumping to Conclusions

TIRED AND UPSET, I jumped out of bed at two a.m. and stomped down the hallway to the front door of our home. Our Cocker Spaniel, Pretty Boy, had been barking for the last half hour and my blood was boiling. Opening the door, I caught Pretty Boy in full bark, standing ten feet away at the end of his chain facing the door.

One look at my face convinced Pretty Boy that he was in serious trouble, so he immediately quit barking and went into his mercy routine, cowering, turning his head to one side and avoiding my angry gaze. I descended the metal grate stairs, held his snout and scolded him, "No more barking!"

My task completed, I climbed back up the stairs, closed the door behind me and headed to my bedroom.

That's when I noticed a strong odor. Funny, I thought, I didn't smell anything earlier.

I climbed in bed and my wife exclaimed, "Phew! What's that smell?"

I answered, "I don't know."

The odor got stronger and stronger and my wife remarked, "It smells like a skunk is in our bed!"

We lifted the covers and an overpowering stench drove us both out of bed. There wasn't a skunk in our bed, but my feet smelled like they were a first cousin to one!

After showering and replacing the sheets I realized what happened. Pretty Boy had been barking at a skunk that was eating his dog food under the metal grated stairs. After I scolded Pretty Boy, the startled skunk sprayed my feet as I climbed up the metal grated stairs to go back in the house.

Pretty Boy had just been doing his job, alerting us to a skunk under our stairs, and I had jumped to the wrong conclusion, because I failed to gather all the facts. As a result, I unjustly punished Pretty Boy and I stunk up our house.

It's easy to jump to conclusions without getting all the facts, isn't it? We're so sure of our case against someone that we lay into them with both barrels, not bothering to listen to their side of the story. Unfortunately, we often find out later that we went off half-cocked and administered our so-called justice to an innocent party. Something smells, then, and it's not a skunk, but our own prejudiced arrogance.

God is concerned with justice and so should we be. Concerning a charge against someone, He required that there be "two or three witnesses" (Mt. 18:16) to verify it. He did not allow His people to jump to conclusions about anyone, even foreigners, concerning justice because it is simply against His nature. As His children, that should be our nature, also.

Another area we jump to conclusions is Biblical truth. John warns us in 1 John 4:1 *"Beloved, do not believe every spirit, but test the spirits to see whether they are from God, for many false prophets have gone out into the world."* The church has been bombarded with new and novel teachings over the centuries that have led people astray and we are not immune to the same danger today. These teachings are either from God or they are from the antichrist and we are to test them to see where they come from.

So, how do we "test the spirits?" 1 John 4:6 says, *"Whoever knows God listens to us; whoever is not from God does not listen to us. By this we know the Spirit of truth and the spirit of error."* John is saying we must test everything by the Word of God that was delivered to us by the Apostles.

Peter confirms this in 2 Peter 1:21 *"For no prophecy was ever produced by the will of man, but men spoke from God as they were carried along by the Holy Spirit."* God used the Apostles to deliver His word accurately and truthfully in the Bible, and it's our responsibility to study the Word so we can discern His truth.

Jesus warned us that *"false christs and false prophets will arise and perform great signs and wonders, so as to lead astray, if possible, even the elect." (Mt. 24:24)* This danger increases as we draw closer to the end of the age, so we need to be vigilant to protect ourselves from these false christs and prophets that want to lead us astray.

Thank God that *"He who is in you is greater than he who is in the world."* (1 Jn 4:4) Devote yourselves to studying God's Word and ask the Holy Spirit to teach you the truth so you can be overcomers. God is faithful and will protect you!

Week 4

Clearing Away the Fog

CLAM SEASON STARTS soon. One summer day, at the age of seven, I reached into a clam hole, pinched the neck of a whopper razor clam and held on for dear life. We battled for what seemed ages, the clam digging for China and me barely holding on. With my arm shoulder deep in the sand and the clam still battling to escape, I finally prevailed and pulled it out of the hole. My victory over that clam seemed to prove my valor, manhood and anything else that needed proving that day. I was hooked on clam digging!

So, when clam season arrived a few years back, I slipped on my tennis shoes, shorts and short-sleeved sweatshirt, (I was taught that real clam diggers don't bother with all that expensive, fancy gear that keeps you warm and dry!), and headed to the beach with my clam gun, (shovel), and clam bag in the annual pursuit of proving my manhood. Oh, and I brought my wife, too, so she could marvel at my skill!

Parking my car at Griffith-Pryday Park, I noticed that the fog was unusually heavy and ... there were no other cars in the parking lot. Strange, I thought, since I wasn't all that early. Maybe I was just lucky and beat the crowd, I reasoned as I walked to the beach. When I neared the surf, I noticed that there not only wasn't a crowd, there wasn't another soul on the beach.

Well, there was one other soul on the beach. It was my wife, who clearly saw fog clouding my brain and asked, "Are you sure this is

19

the right day to dig?" Driving her point home, she added, "Why isn't anyone else digging?"

"Maybe they don't like to dig in the fog," I said politely, but I was really thinking, "*Women! They don't understand anything!*" Then I reasoned to myself, "*I'm already here, so I'm digging!*" And I did, all by myself, with my wife standing at a distance, afraid to associate with me, worried that a dozen game wardens would come charging out of the fog, confiscate my clam gun and clams, handcuff me and lead me off to clam diggers jail.

You're probably thinking I dug on the wrong day and got a ticket. Well, I did dig on the wrong day, but I didn't get a ticket. Whether the fog hid me from the game wardens or they just stayed home that day, I don't know.

The truth was, I erred because I didn't know clam digging had been delayed one day on our beach. My ignorance and stubbornness could have caused me grief and cost me money (For penance, I skipped a day of digging).

Isn't that the way it often is? Aren't many of our troubles and problems a result of error because we just didn't know? I think so. For example: "Really officer, I thought the speed limit was 50, not 35"; "My kids would never do that (insert situation)!"; or my favorite, "If I had known I was going to live this long, I would have taken better care of myself."

Sadly, being in error doesn't change the consequences of our actions. We all have the responsibility to make good choices based on facts, not fancy. Being wrong is wrong, no matter what our excuse.

Jesus emphasized this truth during His last week in Jerusalem. (Mt 22) The Sadducees tried to trap Him with a trick question on marriage in heaven. A woman had been married to seven brothers and they asked Jesus whose wife she would be in heaven. After explaining there is no marriage in heaven, Jesus told them, "*You are in error because you do not know the Scriptures or the power of God.*" (Mt. 22:29) These are the two root causes of most, if not all, of our problems. We haven't discovered the truth of God's Word.

As I look back on my life, I recognize how I mishandled problems because I didn't know how to apply God's Word to my situations. Even though I read, studied, memorized and preached His Word, I often didn't apply 2 Timothy 3:16 to my life situations. Paul told Timothy, *"All Scripture is God-breathed and is useful for teaching, rebuking, correcting and training in righteousness, so that the man of God may be thoroughly equipped for every good work."*

God's Word teaches us "what's right and not right and how to get right."

Being in error concerning God's ways is no excuse and will not protect us from the attacks of the devil and the allure of the world and the foolishness of our sinful nature. God has given us His Word and we are without excuse. Take time to discover the truth in God's Word. Read it, study it, and apply it as if your life depends on it, because it does. May God deliver us from error.

Week 5

Something Special

THE CAMAS PRAIRIE IN northcentral Idaho almost defies description. Containing some of the richest farmland in the world, it sits high above the Clearwater River on the north, the South Fork of the Clearwater River on the east, the Salmon River on the south and the Snake River on the west.

Jim Jessup farmed several thousand acres on the prairie north of Grangeville, employing several farmhands who lived on his property. One Saturday he and his whole crew, including their wives and children, gathered behind the barn to vaccinate the new dairy calves.

About an hour into their project Jim asked, "Has anyone seen little Luis?"

Someone answered, "I saw him in front of the barn about an hour ago.

"I'll go look for him." He came back a few minutes later and reported, "I didn't see Luis anywhere!" Everyone stopped what they were doing and frantically searched for three-year-old Luis.

They never found Luis that day, or any other day. There were many theories about what happened to Luis, but most believed that little Luis wandered into the pig pen and was eaten by the voracious hogs.

Jim Jessup, devasted by the loss, quickly descended into a deep depression. He sat in his rocker hours on end, looking out the window mourning their loss, unable to adjust to the tragedy. One morning Jim's wife got up and noticed that Jim wasn't in his rocker. "Has anyone seen Jim?" she asked her family.

No one had that morning, so they quickly organized a search for Jim. A half hour later they found him in the big barn, wandering around, mumbling, looking for baling twine to hang himself. Miraculously, there was no twine to be found in the barn that morning.

Jim was led back to the house, where his brother in law Larry shared the hope that is in the Gospel of Jesus Christ. Jim surrendered his life to Jesus that day and slowly climbed out of the depression pit he had been mired in. He later became an elder in the Cottonwood Community Church and was a tireless volunteer with the Gideons.

Years later, when I was pastoring the Cottonwood Church, Jim called and asked if I could help with his haying the next day. "Sure," I answered, "Is it okay if I bring my son Jeremy with me?" "No problem," Jim replied.

Ten-year-old Jeremy and I arrived at Jim's farm the next morning ready to work. Jim pulled a large hay wagon with his tractor, I threw the hay bales onto the wagon, and Jeremy did what he could to stack the bales. As we moved from one pile of bales to another, I walked alongside the wagon and Jeremy sat on the tongue that covered the front wheel.

When Jim came to a stop, Jeremy yelled, "Help, Dad!"

Alarmed, I ran to the front of the hay wagon and saw Jeremy's foot turned at a hideous angle, wedged inside of a small opening over the wheel. His foot had somehow slipped into the opening and the wheel caught it as Jim came to a stop. If Jim had gone even a couple of more inches before stopping, Jeremy's foot would have been ripped off. I tried pulling Jeremy's foot out, but it wouldn't budge.

When Jim ran back to see what was wrong, I told him, "You're going to have to back the tractor up so we can get Jeremy's foot out." Jim ran to the tractor, backed up about three inches, and Jeremy's foot came out. We were so shaken by this near disaster we quit work and headed home, thinking about what could have happened.

Half way home, Jeremy turned to me and said, "Dad, I think God has something special he wants me to do for Him."

I reflected a moment and answered, "Yes, I think you're right."

Sometimes we feel that we are not special to God, that He can't use us. We feel paralyzed by our failures and sense of inadequacy, sitting on the sidelines watching life go by. When we feel this way, we need to remember the times in our lives that God protected us. When we recognize God's intervention in our lives, it frees us from the crippling fear of regret and reminds us that God saved us for a purpose - to use us for His glory.

When David faced the giant Goliath, he told his doubters, *"The Lord who delivered me from the paw of the lion and the paw of the bear will deliver me from the hand of this Philistine."* (1 Sam. 17:37) Hearing this, King Saul told David, *"Go, and the Lord be with you!"* He remembered God's grace in his life.

In the same way, you and I need to remember and celebrate God's miraculous interventions in our lives. When we thank Him for His mighty power working in us, I believe we will hear Him whisper to our hearts, "You are something special to Me." Go, and the Lord be with you!

Week 6

Footholds

DEVIL'S TOWER IN WYOMING is an impressive sight. The 867-foot-high rock shaft looms high over the surrounding countryside and is visible for as far away as 100 miles. The top of the tower is over 5,112 feet in elevation. Made of igneous rock, there are several theories on how it was formed, but there is no consensus. Native Americans, who consider it sacred, call it Bear Lodge Butte and perform many religious ceremonies there each year.

If you walk the path around the base of the Tower, as we did on a vacation, you are surprised to see rock climbers above you at different elevations on the rock shaft. We learned later that thousands of climbers make it to the top each year. Some of the climbing routes are considered easy, while a few routes are considered some of the hardest in the world. What looked like an impossible barrier to us was actually a well-traveled path to the top for the experienced rock climber.

Although Devil's Tower appears to be a sheer rock wall from a distance, there are actually many cracks, crevices and small ledges. The rock climber uses these imperfections in the wall as footholds for his ascent to the top.

The Devil is much like a rock climber in his attempt to conquer us. He walks around the base of our lives looking for imperfections (sins) to use as footholds to conquer us. His goal is to 'steal, kill and destroy' us and sin gives him the leverage he needs to conquer us. That is why Ephesians 4:27 warns us, *"do not give the devil a foothold."* What kind of foothold is Satan looking for? The one associated with Ephesians 4:27 is anger. When we get angry and lose our temper, we give Satan a foothold in our life. He uses our anger to hurt others and ourselves, often with irreparable consequences. All of us can remember a time when we hurt someone else, or they hurt us, when anger resulted in harmful words or actions. Satan used that anger to win a victory over our lives.

Lack of self-control is another foothold that Satan loves. He uses our lack of self-control to bury us under an avalanche of impulsive actions and bad habits. We've all faced the frustration of trying to escape the prison these impulsive actions or bad habits have constructed in our lives. No matter how desperate we are, we seem helpless to escape them.

What other footholds does Satan use to conquer us? The list is long and includes greed, lust, selfishness, bitterness, unforgiveness, immorality, fear, lying, laziness and many others. We do our best to hide these imperfections from others, but Satan is an expert at finding the cracks and crevices in our lives and he uses them to gain victory over us.

How do we deny Satan a foothold in our lives? James instructs us, *"Submit yourselves, then, to God. Resist the devil and he will flee from you. Humble yourselves before the Lord, and He will lift you up."* (James 4:7, 10) These verses tell us that it is impossible for us to defeat the Devil on our own. We must position ourselves with God in a way that He wins the victory for us.

We see two steps to victory in these verses:

First, we submit to God, and humble ourselves before Him, admitting we are weak and helpless, incapable of defeating the Devil on our own. When the Holy Spirit brings conviction of sin and we agree with God, asking Him to do what we cannot, it allows God's grace to work in our lives. By submitting and humbling ourselves before God, we essentially say, "God, I've tried it my way and it hasn't worked. I give You control of my life." God always does his part!

Second, we 'resist the devil'. This is not a passive "let go and let God" tactic, but a passionate resistance towards the Devil. We use the Sword of the Spirit, the Word of God, to fight against the temptations that Satan uses against us. Romans 6:11-14 says,

> *"In the same way, count yourselves dead to sin but alive to God in Christ Jesus. Therefore, do not let sin reign in your mortal body so that you obey its evil desires. Do not offer the parts of your body to sin, as instruments of wickedness, but rather offer yourselves to God, as those who have been brought from death to life; and offer the parts of your body to Him as instruments of righteousness. For sin shall not be your master, because you are not under law, but under grace."*

This means we remember Who we belong to and why we are here. We aren't here to please our flesh, but to serve the living God. We do that by offering ourselves daily as living sacrifices, instruments of righteousness. When we do this, the devil flees and God lifts us up, giving us victory over the sin so that easily entangles us. May God give you the victory!

Week 7

Choosing Sides

THE BATTLE BETWEEN David and Goliath is the classic example of the little guy winning despite overwhelming odds against him. Did you know that it is also one of the Bible's clearest pictures of the Gospel of Jesus Christ?

The account of David fighting Goliath is found in *1 Samuel 17*. Since you are probably familiar with the story, I won't repeat it here except to point out the stakes that were involved in the battle.

Israel and the Philistines were lined up on opposite sides of the Valley of Elah, which is a quarter mile wide with a small stream meandering through it. Natural enemies, Israel and the Philistines constantly fought each other for supremacy. If Israel lost, they became slaves of the Philistines. If Israel won, they gained their freedom and independence.

David and Goliath, as the selected champions of their respective armies, carried the burden of national victory or defeat on their shoulders that day. When they met in that small valley for personal combat, each army was vitally concerned about the outcome because it would personally affect all of them before the day was over.

Can you imagine the men of those two armies as they watched David and Goliath approaching each other? Can't you just see the Philistine's licking their lips as their hardened war veteran, the nine-foot tall Goliath, lumbered towards his young, inexperienced opponent? Overconfidence would have been an understatement as they anticipated their champion's sure victory.

On the opposite side of the valley, the Israelites must have had a look of stunned disbelief on their faces as they watched the unknown shepherd boy run towards Goliath. He had no weapons except a staff, a sling and five smooth stones and he couldn't have inspired any confidence for Israel that day. You can almost feel their fear as they envisioned a hasty retreat when the grisly lop-sided battle would quickly be over. If they would have had track shoes, they would have been putting them on in preparation for their headlong flight from their enemies

We know, of course, that the looks on the faces of each army changed when David, who depended on the "Name of the Lord Almighty", triumphed over Goliath. When the Philistines saw that their hero was dead, they fled, and the Israelites pursued them to the gates of their cities. Because they were on David's side, all Israel shared in David's victory that day.

When David fought Goliath, it was a picture of Jesus Christ fighting Satan at Calvary. As Jesus hung on that cruel cross, naked, bleeding and dying, it appeared to all the world that Satan was the victor that day. The disciples ran and hid, fearing that they would meet the same fate as Jesus.

The Resurrection proved that Jesus won the victory over Satan, though. *Colossians 2:15* states, *"And having disarmed the powers and authorities, He made a public spectacle of them, triumphing over them by the cross."* Because Jesus loved us, He carried our sin to the cross and paid our penalty, death, so He could give eternal life to all who believe in Him. Jesus now reigns from Heaven and we are waiting His return, when Satan and sin will completely be destroyed forever.

The victory has been won and the only issue now is whose side are we on – Satan's or Christ's. The Gospel only becomes Good News when we choose to align ourselves with Jesus Christ. By giving ourselves completely to Him, we are saying, "I believe you fought and won the battle for me. I surrender my life to follow You. I am no longer in control of my destiny and I put my life under Your control." In short, we put our faith in Jesus Christ and choose to follow Him. He reigns in our lives as Lord and Savior

Again, the issue is, whose side are you on? The World, with its impressive assortment of allurements, seems to have the upper hand, but it is a temporary allusion. Jesus Christ is coming again and He will judge the whole earth. If you reject Jesus Christ as your Savior and Lord, you will eventually die and stand before Him, be forced to proclaim Him Lord, and suffer the fate of all who have rejected Him, which is the second death.

If, on the other hand, you chose to follow Christ, He will welcome you into His Kingdom, where sin, sickness and death have been vanquished. *"No eye has seen, no ear has heard, no mind has conceived what God has prepared for those who love Him"* - but God has revealed it to us by His Spirit.

Victory or defeat depends on who you choose to be your champion. Choose Jesus Christ and share His victory over sin and death.

Week 8

Mercy Please

ONE SUMMER AFTERNOON my mom was fitting the 'hurried, hectic housewife syndrome' perfectly, and I wasn't helping the situation with my nine-year-old antics. I'm not sure which straw finally broke the camel's back, but I clearly crossed the line of my mom's patience and tolerance when she suddenly threatened, "When your father gets home, you're going to get a spanking!"

This was a sobering revelation, since my dad was due home any minute. Visions of his heavy black leather belt crashing against my little white behind sent shivers up and down my spine. I knew I was in big trouble.

When my dad's car entered our driveway, my mom flew out the door with her message of doom. Moments later, she followed my dad through the door with a triumphant look on her face, knowing justice would be done.

My dad angrily confronted me and asked, "What have you got to say for yourself, young man?"

Almost whimpering, knowing that I was guilty as charged and without an excuse, I answered, "Nothing, sir."

"Okay, into your bedroom," he commanded as he pulled out his shiny black belt, which looked like a bullwhip to my fearful eyes, and gave it a couple of practice swings. As I fearfully headed down the hallway to my room, I looked back at my mom, whose eyes almost gleamed, knowing that I would finally get what I deserved. As for my eyes, they were already forming tears as I laid face down on the bed and waited for that first lightning stab of pain on my rear end.

Then, to my surprise, my dad whispered, "When I hit the bed with my belt, you holler."

I stared at my dad incredulously and, then, with a smile of comprehension, I nodded. "Okay."

That was the worst beating my old bed ever got and the best lesson I ever learned from my dad. You see, sometimes a little mercy goes a long way at critical times in a person's life. Knowing what I deserved, and didn't get, this was one of those times.

Somehow, my disobedience and my dad's mercy led me to a greater love and appreciation of my dad that day.

You and I are sinners by nature and God, who is a Holy God, must punish sinners, which includes you and I, for our sin. The Bible declares that the penalty for sin is death and that is exactly what we deserve, since we are all sinners. If God were to overlook even one sin, He would not be Holy and there would be no real justice in our world.

It is true that God is Holy, but it is also true that He is merciful. Over and over in the Bible God shows that He is a merciful God. Just the fact that you and I are still here speaks to God's mercy since He should have reached out to destroy us the moment we first sinned. God's mercy flows from God's love and leads to God's grace for everyone who looks to Christ for salvation.

Although God's grace is free, it isn't cheap. Jesus Christ purchased our pardon from sin when He went to the cross in our place, paying for our sins with His own blood, dying in our place. He has satisfied, or propitiated, God's wrath by taking it upon Himself for us. God demonstrated His love!

You may be feeling 'guilty as charged' and unworthy of forgiveness, but God is anxious to pour out His mercy on you. No matter what sin you've committed, or how many, God longs to restore you to a loving relationship with Him. That's why God sent His only Son Jesus to die in our place on the cross. When we make Jesus our Savior and Lord, He treats us as children who need training instead of rebels who deserve justice. Since this is true, the writer to the Hebrews encourages us, *"Let us then approach the throne of grace with confidence, so that we may receive mercy and find grace to help us in our time of need." (Hebrews 4:16)*

How should we respond to God's mercy? The Apostle Paul advises us, *"Therefore, I urge you, brothers, in view of God's mercy, to offer your bodies as living sacrifices, holy and pleasing to God – which is your Spiritual worship." (Romans 12:1)*

If you will do this, you will find that a little mercy goes a long way in living a life that is pleasing to our Heavenly Father. You will also discover that God's love for you satisfies the longing of your heart as nothing else will.

Week 9

Are You Sure About That?

IN THE LATE 1980'S I was the part-time chaplain at the Northern Idaho Correctional Institute. The Sergeant there had a four-year-old boy, named Bobby, that my wife and I baby sat when he was working. Bobby hadn't been disciplined much, and he often proved to be a real handful for us.

We had been watching Bobby for about a month when he fell at home and broke his arm. They casted his arm and it didn't seem to slow him down at all. A week later, our son Jeremy fell out of the tree in front of our house and broke his arm, so he had a cast, too. Now when someone comes to visit your house and they see a boy with a cast on his arm, they think, "Accident," right? When they see two boys with casts on their arms, well, you can guess what they are thinking!

One Saturday we were watching Bobby when the kids asked if they could go outside to play. Bobby wanted to play, too, so I volunteered to go watch them. I decided to mow the grass while I watched the boys and they went from the front yard to the back, chasing each other and having fun.

About fifteen minutes later a car turned onto our street and pulled up in front of our house. The driver rolled his window down, so I walked over to see what he wanted. His wife was in the passenger seat and there were kids in the back. "Have you seen little Bobby," he asked?

"He's in the back yard playing with my boys," I answered.

"Are you sure about that?" he asked.

"Yes, I'm sure," I said, nodding my head up and down. "I just saw him a few minutes ago."

The look on the man's face changed and he pointed angrily at me, "Bobby's not in your back yard. He's in the back seat of my car!" Incredulous, I looked in the back of the car and there was Bobby! With no pants on!

Turns out Bobby had pooped his pants while playing with my boys, so he decided to go home, which was on the other side of town. The couple in the car had found him walking on the side of the road about 4 blocks away, carrying his poopy pants. Needless to say, I was pretty embarrassed.

Before you question my childrearing abilities, I have to say, I've watched hundreds of kids over the years and I'm sure they're all still alive. Well, I'm pretty sure they all survived!

Often, the things we are sure about aren't sure things, are they? How many times have we said," I'm sure I can do this," and we couldn't? How many times have we said, "I'll never do that", and we did. The truth is, we tend to overestimate our strengths and underestimate our weaknesses. Usually it's no big deal. We learn from our mistakes and move on in life.

There is one mistake in life that we can never recover from, though. Are we sure that we have eternal life? Is there any way we can know for sure? What are some signs that we actually do have eternal life?

John wrote 1 John to answer these questions. He says in 1 John 5:13, *"I write these things to you who believe in the name of the Son of God so that you may know that you have eternal life."* The word know is an experiential know. It's not knowing about something, but knowing it so well that you are one hundred percent sure. Eternal life is too important to not know for sure.

What are "*these things*"? John discussed **four things** in this letter:

First, there was faith in Christ. This isn't an intellectual faith, but an experiential faith, where we trust Jesus with our lives. This includes believing the truth about Jesus, but it also means following Jesus.

Second, there was love for God. If we say we love God, that means He comes first in our lives. Jesus said, *"Whoever finds his life will lose it, and whoever loses his life for my sake will find it."* The true Christian puts God first in his or her life. We worship him, not ourselves or anyone else.

Third, there was love for our Christian brothers and sisters. If we have been born of God, then we are members of the same family. We should love to be around other Christians. John says if we say we love God and hate our brothers, we are liars.

Last, there is a love for God's commands. We believe that all God's commands for us are for our good. They are not *'burdensome'* for the Christian. John says, *"This is love for God, to obey His commands."* (1 Jn 5:3)

Are you sure you have eternal life?

Week 10

The Smoke of Their Torment

WE'VE SEEN AN ABUNDANCE of wild fires recently. Two summers ago, fires in Canada filled our Western Washington skies with smoke. Last summer, fires from Canada and Eastern Washington almost blotted out the sun the month of August. When we drove to Alaska, we didn't see clear skies until we reached Whitehorse, Yukon. Recently we watched two California fires with dread as they caused the terrible destruction of homes and the tragic loss of lives. The Governor of California recently commented that this is "the new normal in the West." Someone else remarked, "It reminds you of Hell."

Unlike Hell, though, these fires are only temporary. Sooner or later, cool weather, with its wind and rain, extinguishes the fires and dissipates the smoke. The grim reminder of blackened ground and charred trees remains, but, eventually, even that is replaced by the green of new growth. The cycle of life goes on.

The real Hell is not temporary, though. Jude speaks of Hell as *"the eternal fire." (Jude 7)* Revelation states that *"the smoke of their torment rises for ever and ever." (Rev. 9:13)* Hell is a real and literal place where those who have rejected Christ will experience unbearable torment and agony for all of eternity. Because of the magnitude of the consequences, Hell isn't an issue that anyone should take lightly.

Someone may ask, "How can a loving God condemn people to Hell, with its suffering and agony?" The answer to that question is simple – God doesn't want anyone to go to Hell. Ezekiel says, "Do I take any pleasure in the death of wicked? declares the Lord. Rather, am I not pleased when they turn from their ways live?" (Ez. 18:23) Peter tells us, *"He is patient with you, not wanting anyone to perish, but everyone to come to repentance." (2 Peter 3:9)*

God has done, and is doing, everything possible to rescue the perishing from Hell. When Jesus died on the cross, He paid in full the penalty that sin incurred for us. Now, through the Holy Spirit, He is drawing men and women to Himself to receive the free gift of salvation. It comes down to this: do you realize your need for salvation and are you willing to accept it on His terms, surrendering your life to Jesus and following Him. If we do this, God not only rescues us from Hell, but He gives us the underserved gift of Heaven.

If we refuse God's offer of salvation through Jesus Christ, Hebrews warns us, *"If we deliberately keep on sinning after we have received the knowledge of the truth, no sacrifice for sins is left, but only a fearful expectation of judgement and raging fire that will consume the enemies of God." (Heb. 10:26-27)* If we refuse God's gracious gift of His Son, he promises us, *"How much more severely do you think a man deserves to be punished, who has trampled the Son of God underfoot, who has treated as an unholy thing the blood of the covenant that sanctified him, and who has insulted the Spirit of grace?" (Heb. 10:29)*

On the other hand, if we put our faith in Jesus and commit our lives to following Him, God graciously saves all who come to Him by faith. Jesus says, *"If anyone loves me, he will obey my teaching. My Father will love him, and we will come to him and make our home with him." (John 14:23)* He promises to give us the Holy Spirit, who guarantees our eternal inheritance with Jesus. *"Amazing love, how can it be that Thou my God shouldst die for me!"* (Amazing Grace, by John Newton)

Already the wind and rain are extinguishing the fires and bringing relief to the residents of California. The only relief for Hell, though, is to never go there. God pleads with us through the Holy Spirit to accept the salvation that His beloved Son won for us on the cross. Jesus cries out, *"If anyone is thirsty, let him come to me and drink. Whoever believes in me, as the Scripture has said, streams of living water will flow from within him."* (John 37-38)

If you have already come to Jesus and know that He has saved you from your sins and Hell, thank Him, love Him, and live for Him. When you do this, you begin to experience God's blessings of Heaven now in this life.

Week 11

Truth or Consequences

OUR RECENT BOUT OF cold weather, with its snow and ice, reminded me of some of the winters I spent in Montana and Idaho.

One winter Old Man Winter came knocking on my door and asked some unpleasant questions. It seems that he plays his own version of the popular game Truth or Consequences.

First, he started nagging me about my woodpile. "Are you sure you cut enough wood last summer?" he chuckled, with a silly grin on his face. I looked at my quickly diminishing woodpile and could only muster a feeble, "I hope so."

Then, with the temperature near zero, he casually asked, "How does your car start in the cold with that old battery?" I went out to ask the car the same question. All it said was "unt-oh, unt-oh, unt-oh" as the starter barely turned over. We wouldn't be going to town or anywhere else until the temperature warmed up a bit.

Finally, Old man Winter added insult to injury one night when he inquired, "Why isn't your water running?" Obviously, he already knew that I forgot to wrap heat tape around my water pipes before the freezing weather came, so I didn't even bother to answer him. I had already learned that when it came to Truth or Consequences, there is no way to fool Old Man Winter.

Last summer the truth about winter seemed far away and unimportant and it was easy to ignore the consequences of being unprepared. When winter finally arrived, though, my failure to plan and prepare came with a price to be paid for ignoring the truth. If we can't fool Old Man Winter, imagine trying to fool God. People ignore God and think they will escape the consequences of their actions. They reason, nothing has happened to me yet, so nothing will happen to me. Peter warns us against this mindset when he says, *"The Lord is not slow in keeping His promise, as some understand slowness. He is patient with you, not wanting anyone to perish, but everyone to come to repentance."* *(2 Peter 3:9)* It is the height of foolishness to think that God doesn't see, doesn't remember and doesn't bring justice.

Whether we realize it or not, all of us will face the consequences of our choices in life, whether wise or foolish, both now and forever. All of us will stand before God one day and play Truth or Consequences. When the book of our lives is opened there will be no lies or excuses, only the truth. God will ask us if we loved His Son Jesus and our answer will be the result of how we responded to Him while we were on this earth. Most respond with indifference. Even if they say, "Yes, I love Jesus," there is nothing in their actions or lives to show that to be the truth. Others may question the depth of their love for Jesus, but God, who knows the thoughts and desires of the heart, will recognize their love for Jesus.

The truth is often inconvenient, but the consequences are always real and inescapable. If we know and love Jesus, the truth is we will spend eternity in heaven with Him. If we do not know and love Jesus, the truth is, we will spend eternity in Hell separated from Him. We can ignore the truth if we want to because it is inconvenient, but this won't change the consequences.

Christ's parable about the ten virgins in Matthew 25 should be enough warning for all of us. The Bridegroom was late in coming and all of the virgins fell asleep. At midnight the cry rang out: *"Here's the bridegroom! Come out to meet him!"* The wise virgins had oil in their lamps and went out to meet the bridegroom, but the foolish virgins had no oil and went looking for oil to purchase. When the foolish virgins finally arrived at the wedding banquet, they found the door shut and cried, *"Sir! Sir! Open the door for us!"* But it was too late and the Bridegroom replied, *"I tell you the truth, I don't know you."*

Jesus advice to all of us is, *"Therefore keep watch, because you do not know the day or the hour."* (Mt. 22:37) The truth is, Jesus is coming back and we have the responsibility to be ready, or else we, too, will face the consequences. Be ready!

Week 12

Where's Santa?

"HURRY HOME!" THE WOMEN cried as my grandpa, uncle and dad left to go find Santa Claus. My brother, cousins and I jumped for joy at the thought of old Saint Nick personally delivering our presents on Christmas Eve.

Waiting patiently, we tried not to annoy our moms and grandma. Still, after playing for a half hour, we couldn't help ourselves and inquired, "How long before Santa comes?"

"Not much longer," they promised us.

Another half hour dragged by and our impatience turned to worry. "What if they can't find Santa," we echoed.

A little less certain, they assured us, "Oh, they'll find him okay. Don't worry." Still, when they picked up the phone and had a heated conversation with the person on the other end, we were more than a little concerned.

It got later and later and, one by one, we kids fell asleep in my grandparents living room.

Finally, two hours after the men left, the slam of a car door and a loud "Ho! Ho! Ho!" outside the house awakened us.

Jumping up in excitement, we gazed as a drunken Santa Claus, with a bag of toys slung over his shoulder, stumbled through the front door into the living room. In our hearts, we knew Santa was really my uncle, who had spent the last two hours drinking with my dad and grandpa at the local tavern, but our youthful excitement somehow overlooked our earlier disappointment.

Drinking was a big part of our family lives and we somehow dealt with it. It wasn't until later in life that we learned the true cost alcohol had imposed on our families – fights, divorces and early deaths.

Christmas is supposed to be a joyous time of year, when families celebrate the birth of Jesus and share their love with each other. Often, though, alcohol and drugs ruin the celebration. Many, by replacing Christmas joy with Christmas party, simply use the holiday as an excuse to indulge their addictions.

Families are affected in many ways. Some waste precious resources (money) on getting high, looking for artificial joy. Others become an embarrassment, saying and doing things that harm family relationships. A few never make it home, dying on our highways under the influence of drink or drugs. More and more, addictions also play a role in suicides, which seem to spike during the Christmas holiday.

It's hard to believe that the excuse for these kinds of bad behavior is the birth of our Savior, Jesus Christ. One can't help but wonder what God thinks about our so-called 'joyous season'. Drunken revelry is bad enough at any time of the year, but it must especially break God's heart when it's done during a holiday that supposedly honors His Son.

We know that the world has hijacked the Christmas holiday that honors the birth of Jesus Christ, but, as Jesus' followers, we need to stay focused on the reason for the celebration. John 3:16 reminds us that *"God so loved the world, that He gave His only Son, that whoever believes in Him should not perish but have eternal life."*

God gave His Son Jesus for our sins, and for those who know Jesus, this should be a time of great thankfulness. The world uses Christmas as a reason to give gifts to each other and even they know the importance of giving thanks. How much more should our hearts overflow with thankfulness at this time of year for what God has given us in His Son.

Even more important than thankfulness, though, is worship, since it is God who has given this amazing gift of His Son to us. Like the shepherds and Wisemen, the birth of Jesus should evoke a strong desire to worship God for His love for us. This should be both private in our homes and corporate in our churches. We sing the Christmas Carols as an act of worship for what God has given to us. Hallelujah!

This year, make a conscious effort to have a truly Merry Christmas by honoring Christ's gift of Himself by giving yourself completely to Him. By giving yourself completely to Christ, you are actually giving yourself the greatest gift of all, an intimate relationship with the One who came into the world to die for you so you can have an abundant life. That is so much greater than whatever high the world can offer you.

Merry Christmas!

Week 13

The Gift

CHRISTMAS JUST ISN'T the same as it used to be for me. When I was little, I got lots and lots of presents. Evidently, my relatives thought I was cute then, because they all sent me a gift for Christmas.

That all changed as I got older, though. I'm not sure why – maybe I wasn't so cute anymore – but every year there were fewer and fewer gifts under the Christmas tree for me. Finally, one year, there was only one gift under the tree with my name on it.

At first, I thought that Santa would bring me some more gifts – but he didn't. Then, I hoped it was an expensive gift – but it wasn't. Finally, I told myself it didn't matter – but it did.

One gift or not, Christmas morning finally arrived and the kids hustled me out to the tree so we could open our gifts. We sat around the tree and the kids watched with anticipation and glee as their pile of presents grew bigger and bigger in front of them. There was a look of concern on their faces when they noticed that I only had one gift in front of me, but they were quickly distracted by their own good fortune and I was left to ponder my one gift alone.

Starting with the youngest, we opened our presents. There were squeals of delight as each child discovered the wonderful gifts that were given to them.

I was genuinely happy for each child's gifts, but I couldn't help but wonder, "What is in that single present for me?" Finally, it was my turn to open my present. With sweaty palms and unsteady nerves, I removed the wrapping paper, pried open the small box and removed my gift.

Looking back, I suppose I wouldn't have felt so bad about the support stockings if they hadn't felt so good on my aging calves. It's just that, at the time, support stockings seemed like a crushing blow to my youthful ego. Now, of course, with an older ego, and much older calves, I still cherish that gift that was given Christmas morning thirty-six years ago.

Christmas is all about giving, isn't it? We give presents to remind each other of the Gift that God gave to each one of us – His only Son. God's Gift never wears out; never gets old; never loses value; never fails to meet our need. God's Gift is the perfect gift because it gives us what we truly need and desire, abundant and eternal life.

Because *"all have sinned and fallen short of the glory of God" (Rom. 3:23),* and *"the wages of sin is death" (Rom. 6:23),* all of us need life and it only comes through Jesus Christ, who is *"the way and the truth and the life." (John 10:10)* John 3:36 tells us, *"Whoever believes in the Son has eternal life, but whoever rejects the Son will not see life, for God's wrath remains on him."* Jesus is the gift of life to all who truly receive Him.

God offers His Son Jesus as a free gift to all who will receive Him into their lives. The gift is free, but it isn't cheap, since Jesus purchased the gift with His own blood and life. Jesus is precious to all who have received Him into their lives because He alone meets the true needs of our hearts.

If we reject God's gift of Jesus, we forfeit eternal life and all that is left is eternal death, which is eternity separated from the goodness of God. We cannot even imagine the torment of the souls of those who have *"trampled underfoot the Son of God and have profaned the blood of the covenant by which He was sanctified, and have outraged the Spirit of grace." (Heb. 10:29)*

"It is a fearful thing to fall into the hands of the living God." (Heb. 10:31)

Have you truly received Jesus Christ as your Lord and Savior? Then thank Him and give Him glory this Christmas as you contemplate His goodness to you.

If Jesus Christ is not your Lord and Savior, then open your heart and receive Him as the One who truly loves you. Only then can you know the real meaning of Christmas. Jesus is the best gift that anyone can ever receive. He alone meets the true needs of our hearts.

Merry Christmas!

Week 14

Call the Professional

FOR THE SECOND TIME in three years we have spent the week after Thanksgiving without water. I won't comment other than to say – sometimes boys and excavators aren't a good match!

Being without water reminded me of another time I had problems with my plumbing, but this time it was on the septic side of the system.

The voice on the phone was urgent. "Come home quick! The sewer is plugged up!" It sounded like a true emergency, so I rushed home convinced I could save the day.

When I reached home, my nose alerted me to the problem before my eyes could confirm it. That stuff that we normally flush down the toilet was now floating about a foot deep in our basement. The temptation to run away from the upcoming battle was very strong at that moment.

The situation called for all-out war. The first attack was made with the toilet plunger, to which the drain gurgled back mockingly, "Is that all you've got!" Next was the "garden hose down the drain" trick, which only got us into deeper trouble, if you know what I mean.

Obviously, more sophisticated equipment was needed, so a sewer "snake" was rented. Even it was repulsed, as it ventured into the drain about twenty feet and refused to go another inch, as if to say, "This is your stinkin' problem, not mine!"

A new line of attack was needed, so I decided to remove the toilet and run the "snake" in there. Unfortunately, that's when the water line to the toilet broke and created a 6-foot geyser in our bathroom. We counterattacked with a ten-minute search for the shut off valve, which was in the basement, and finally brought the geyser under control.

That's when the rest of the troops arrived home from school. "We have to go to the bathroom!" they cried in unison. No help there.

Unconditional surrender was our only option - we called a professional.

The plumber arrived quickly, surveyed the situation and muttered, "Roots." He walked back to his truck, grabbed his roto-rooter, stuck it down the drain and within minutes the cesspool in our basement began to subside. The plumber mumbled again, "$150", packed up his roto-rooter, headed off to save other amateurs like us, and we were left to begin our mop-up operation. We were drained, but at least there would be a fresher tomorrow.

There's a lesson to be learned from our 'little problem'. Sometimes we encounter problems in life that we aren't trained or properly equipped to handle. We sincerely want to fix the problem, but it just seems bigger than the meager knowledge or resources we have. The problem may be marital, financial, emotional, physical, mental, relational, or spiritual. Whatever the problem, it seems to be just beyond our ability to fix it. Sometimes, despite our best efforts, the problem actually gets worse the more we attack it.

That's when it's time to call in the Professional, Jesus Christ. He not only knows us, since He is our Creator, but He also knows everything we go through, since He experienced what we experience when He walked on this earth. We can call on Him because He cares for you.

David, who experienced many problems, confirms this:

"In my distress I called to the Lord; I cried to my God for help. He reached down from on high and took hold of me; He drew me out of deep waters. He rescued me from my powerful enemy, from my foes, who were too strong for me." (Psalm 18:6,16-17)

Why wait until you are up to your neck in 'stuff' before you call the Professional? James tells us,

> *"If any of you lack wisdom, let him ask God, who gives generously to all without reproach, and it will be given to him. But let him ask in faith, with no doubting, for the one who doubts is like a wave of the sea, that is driven and tossed by the wind. For that person must not suppose that he will receive anything from the Lord; he is a double-minded man, unstable in all of his ways."* (James 1:5-8)

When you experience problems in your life, don't wait - call on the Lord! He can deliver, lead you and give you a fresh tomorrow.

Week 15

For Back Seat Drivers

MY GRANDMOTHER WAS a classic backseat driver. Through commitment to excellence and faithfulness to the basics, she never lost her effectiveness. If you are a backseat driver, here are a few of her time-tested principles that will help you excel in your role as backseat driver.

First, never be pressured into driving. An irritable and abusive driver may challenge you, "If you think you can do a better job, why don't you drive!" Don't fall for this cheap and deceitful trick to trade places with you. No matter how righteous and indignant the driver seems, all he or she really wants is what you have – real power!

Second, never relax. By maintaining constant nervousness and tenseness, you won't lose your effectiveness. When approaching a stoplight, even if it is green, push down hard on the floor to alert the driver to any possible danger at the intersection. If rounding a corner, lean hard in the direction of the turn, warning the driver to slow down, or else! These simple maneuvers will alert the driver to their overconfidence and recklessness.

Third, maintain a sharp lookout for possible dangers. How can you warn the driver about the light that turned yellow four blocks away if you don't see it? How will the driver prepare for evasive action if you don't point out the car that entered the road a mile in the distance? Obviously, without your diligence and assistance, the driver would be placing both of you in great danger, so never fall asleep on your self-appointed watch.

Finally, never become discouraged. Many drivers resent your role and will verbally attack you because of your persistent refusal to ignore potential dangers. To fight off discouragement, simply ignore their ranting and raving and continue doing what you do best, giving unwanted advice to keep the driver on his or her toes in a chaotic world. Any backseat driver worth his or her salt won't let an uninformed and edgy driver keep them from their self-appointed role in life - master of the road ahead!

As I mentioned, my grandmother was an expert backseat driver. During one trip, she was operating at peak performance when my grandfather threatened, "If you don't shut up, I'm going to get out and walk!"

Someone of lesser ability, stamina and vision might have wavered, but not my grandmother – she just kept chattering away. When my grandfather pulled the car over to the side of the freeway, got out and started walking, she wasn't even fazed. She rolled down the passenger window, scooted over into the driver's seat and continued berating him through the open window.

Recognizing defeat, my grandfather threw up his arms, walked around to the driver's side, got back behind the wheel and they continued their trip, safely reaching their destination because of my grandmother's commitment to excellence.

All humor aside, backseat driving often proves one thing – some people excel at criticism above all else. No matter what, these people operate with a superior attitude that says, "No matter what you do, you can never do it as good as they think you should." Negative and critical, they rarely shift into a positive and helpful gear. Their expertise is in tearing down, not building up. Once they turn their attention to you, there is no way you can succeed in their eyes.

Jesus Christ experienced this same kind of criticism. In analyzing His distractors, Jesus compared them to *". . . children sitting in the marketplace and calling out to each other: 'We played the flute for you, and you did not dance; we sang a dirge, and you did not cry.'" (Luke 7:32)* He was saying, some people are impossible to please.

When we are criticized, how should we react?

First, pray and ask God if He is trying to point something out to you. We are told to examine ourselves. It may even be wise to ask a trusted friend if they see the same things in us.

Second, we should make the right response. If we sense there is some truth in the criticism, take the necessary actions to change or improve. If we feel we are innocent of the charges, continue doing what is right and trust God to vindicate you. God's destination for you is Christ-likeness and He can use that backseat driver, whether negative or positive, to help us keep our eyes on the goal.

If we keep our eyes on the goal, not allowing anyone or anything to distract us, we will reach God's destination for us safely.

Week 16

Do I Hafta?

I RECENTLY RECEIVED a letter from a young girl that asked, "Does a Christian have to go to church?" This is a great question that many have asked over the years. It's also a question that often reveals our hearts.

There are essentially two parts to this question:

#1 – Why is it important that Christians go to church?

#2 – Does going to church make us a Christian?

I'll try to answer these questions in two ways – theologically and practically.

First, the theological reason. Hebrews 10:25 commands us, *"Let us not give up meeting together, as some are in the habit of doing, but let us encourage one another – and all the more as you see the Day approaching."* God gives this command, (not a suggestion!), because He knows the Christian life is often hard, especially when times are tough or we face temptations. We meet together to encourage each other in our faith. Giving and receiving encouragement requires that we see each other, listen to each other, and pray for each other. Obviously, none of these things can happen if we don't meet together with the intention of getting to know each other better.

John approaches this issue from the point of loving each other. He says, *"For anyone who does not love his brother, whom he has seen, cannot love God, whom he has not seen. And he has given us this command:*

Whoever loves God must also love his brother." (1 John 4:20-21) One of the signs that marks Christians is a love for their Christian family. If I have no desire to be with my Christian brother or sister, how can I claim I love them? We express our love for God by loving others, especially Christians. If we say we love God but don't love other Christians, then we are fooling ourselves, and God actually calls us "liars".

Second, the practical answer. It's easy to convince ourselves that we are something when we're not, so we need proof. For example, if I say that I am a basketball player, how can I know that for sure? The obvious answer is - I actually play basketball! Playing basketball requires a basketball court of some kind, usually a gym or outdoor court, and other players. So, if I am a basketball player, I will go to the basketball court and play basketball with other basketball players. Going to the basketball court doesn't make me a basketball player (just like going to church doesn't make me a Christian), but it is something that a real basketball player does because that is who he is.

God taught me the importance of going to church forty years ago. Until then I attended church regularly, but often missed if I felt something was more important, such as ball tournaments and family gatherings. One Saturday night, I took my family to the drive-in theatre to see *Jungle Boy*. There were two movies, so we didn't get home until 1:30 a.m. The next day I sat in church, desperately trying to stay awake to listen to the message, when I felt the Holy Spirit speak to me, saying, "This is the most important event of your week and you can't even stay awake because you stayed out so late last night." I realized I was not giving God my best and I decided to honor Him by going to bed at a decent time on Saturday nights and not to miss church unless it was a real emergency. I understood this didn't make me a Christian, but it was something that I wanted to do to please God.

A few Sunday's later my commitment was tested. My dad called me on a Saturday inviting me to a family picnic the next day in Shelton. My brother would be there, too, so I asked, "What time will the picnic be?" When he said, "Ten a.m."

I told him, "I can't make it."

"Why not?" he asked.

"Because I don't get out of church until noon."

My dad then challenged me, "Which is more important, your family or church?"

I answered calmly," God and my commitment to Him."

We had the family picnic the next day at 1:30 pm.

I can only remember missing church twice in the last forty years (I was traveling and couldn't find a church to attend. I may have been sick once or twice, but can't remember for sure). Even those two times, we stopped, sang a song or two, read some Scripture and prayed. I don't say this with pride, but with thanksgiving that God allowed me to fulfil my pledge to Him.

A pastor told me this story. A member of his church near Denver said he would miss church Sunday because his brother, who loved fishing, was visiting. They were going fishing at a lake high in the Rockies and he was hoping for a chance to witness to him. He had the opportunity to share Jesus, but his brother's response shattered him. "If God was really so important to you, you would be in church today." Ouch!

I don't have to go to church, and it certainly doesn't make me a Christian because I do, but I love meeting with other Christians to worship God, and I have certainly been encouraged because of it. May you be encouraged, too!

Week 17

Don't Let Loose

DISTRACTIONS CAN KEEP you from reaching your goal and winning the prize. This truth was clearly demonstrated to me at a youth wrestling match I attended with my boys many years ago in McCall, Idaho.

A coach of one of the wrestlers at the meet told me the following story. He sighed, "My boy was ahead by one point with less than thirty seconds to go. He was on top and all he had to do was hold on for the win."

Then, with a look of disbelief, he explained what happened. "There was ten seconds left in the match and he had full control of his opponent when his headgear slipped over his face. He let go of his opponent," the coach lamented, "to adjust his headgear, and his opponent used the opportunity to flip my boy over on mat. With just a few seconds left, he pinned my boy and won the match." Exasperated, he added, "He had the match won until he let loose of his opponent to adjust his head gear."

Through inexperience or ignorance, the young wrestler lost sight of his goal (to win the match) because of a minor distraction (his headgear). Unfortunately, we see the same kind of thing happening to many people in everyday life.

For example, a young couple may be doing well in marriage. They are weathering the trials and hardships of marriage when, suddenly, a distraction enters the picture and throws them flat on their backs for a big loss. Losing sight of the goal of a strong and viable marriage, they may have been distracted by an unkind word, or an outside interest, or an unspoken fear. Whatever it is, they may lose their marriage and their testimony as a result.

It can happen in the area of finances. Maybe the goal is financial responsibility and security. Along comes the distraction of a new car, or a vacation, or almost anything outside of the budget. By not keeping the goal in sight, many dig a financial hole that they can't get out of.

It could be a young person that wants to honor God with their lives by committing to wait for a Christian partner. They meet someone who is not living for the glory of Christ, allow an attraction to grow, and, then, they compromise by entering into a relationship that is not God centered. Not only does an unequally yoked marriage create tremendous stress in their marriage, but their kids suffer because they are sending mixed messages to their children.

We fight this same battle spiritually, too. God wants us to become like His Son Jesus Christ, preparing us to spend eternity with Him, when a worldly distraction causes us to wander spiritually. In writing to young Timothy, Paul warns him about those *"who have shipwrecked their faith"* because they lost sight of the goal. Paul advises Timothy and us,

> *"But you, man of God, flee from all this, and pursue righteousness, godliness, faith, love, endurance and gentleness. Fight the good fight of the faith. Take hold of the eternal life to which you were called when you made your good confession in the presence of many witnesses." (1 Timothy 6:11-12)*

Paul's telling us, if your goal is to spend eternity with God, then **hold onto** the good things God has shown you and run away from the distractions that tempt you. This is good advice for us!

What is your goal in life? Does it honor God? Does it have meaning for both now and forever? Then don't let loose of it! Remind yourself daily where you are headed and don't let distractions blow you of course.

If you don't have a worthy goal, then cry out to God and search until you find something worth living for. Don't look in the trash heap of this world for a goal that has no ultimate meaning, but seek those things that are above, that last and have meaning for all of eternity. Put Jesus Christ first in your life and ask Him to direct your steps. He will guide you into a meaningful, satisfying, fulfilling life.

"Let us hold unswervingly to the hope we profess, for He who promised is faithful." (Hebrews 10:23)

Week 18

All About Tents

THE TRAINING WAS TOUGH, but at least it made me an expert. What kind of an expert? Well, an expert on tents. We slept in a tent with our four kids during a 2-week vacation in British Columbia many years ago and I learned everything there is to know about tents.

What did I learn about tents? Well, here's what I learned: tents are cold; and hot; and crowded; and not very private. Then there is the ground you put tents on – it's hard and it seems to get harder the longer you sleep on it. Oh, yes, and don't forget the joy of packing and unpacking the tent every morning and evening. Even though it was fun for a while and remained bearable the whole trip, tent living gave me a whole new appreciation for a warm, snug home with a comfortable bed in it. Living in a tent for 2 weeks taught me that I don't want to be living in a tent permanently!

The Bible describes our bodies at a tent – "For we know that if the tent that is our earthly home is destroyed, we have a building from God, a house not made with hands, eternal in the heavens. For in this tent we groan, longing to put on our heavenly dwelling, if indeed by putting it on we may not be found naked. For while we are still in this tent, we groan, being burdened – not that we would be unclothed, but that we would be further clothed, so that what is mortal may be swallowed up by life. He who has prepared us for this very thing is God, who has given us the Spirit as a guarantee." (2 Cor. 5:1-5)

This body that takes up so much of our time and attention is only a temporary lodging place for our soul. It serves its function well, but it was never meant to be our permanent home. Its only purpose is to provide our soul shelter until we finally reach our eternal destination, which is either heaven or hell.

Abraham understood this truth. "By faith he made his home in the promised land like a stranger in a foreign country; he lived in tents . . . For he was looking forward to the city with foundations, whose architect and builder is God." (Heb. 11:9, 10) Abraham realized the transitory nature of this life and admitted that he was "an alien and stranger" here on this earth (Heb. 11:13) His quest for life could have been power, prestige and pleasure, but we're told, "Instead, they (he) were looking for a better country – a heavenly one. Therefore, God is not ashamed to be called their God, for He has prepared a city for them." (Heb11:16)

Are you "longing for a better country," or are you so caught up with this "earthly tent" that you have lost sight of your eternal destination? If your life is caught up in "tents," I have one more piece of information to pass on to you about them. Tents are flimsy and wear out sooner or later, no matter how well built or fancy they are. They don't last!

Today, if you realize the temporary nature of your "tent," focus your eyes and Jesus Christ and seek His "city with a foundation" that He offers to all who love Him and come to Him in simple faith.

Week 19

Mud Puddles

BAREFOOT AND EAGER to splash in the ocean waves, our boys rushed ahead of us down the trail from our cabin to the beach. When I yelled, "Wait for us in the dunes!", they nodded in agreement before disappearing around a bend in the trail.

Rounding that same corner, we found two-year-old Jeremy playing contentedly in a big, brown mud puddle in the middle of the trail. Seeing us, he smiled as if to say, "This is great fun!"

We encouraged him to keep going on to the beach, but he kept playing in the mud puddle, not willing to go any further. His attitude seemed to be, "A mud puddle in the hand is worth two oceans by the beach."

"The ocean waves are more fun," I coaxed, but his mud puddle enthusiasm wasn't dampened.

"I'll leave you all alone," I threatened, but his mud puddle determination remained unwavering.

"I'll give you a piggyback ride," I promised, but his mud puddle attraction continued strong.

Finally, giving up on childhood psychology, I grabbed his hand and forced him down the trail to the beach. When we crossed over the top of the last dune and he glimpsed the ocean waves, he let go of my hand and raced across the sand to frolic with his brothers in the white, frothy waves. Even big, nice mud puddles lose their allurement when compared with a magnificent blue ocean and its dazzling beauty.

There is much in this world that attracts us, but it pales in comparison to the glory that awaits all who travel with God to the end of the road. God gives His good gifts in this life to encourage and refresh us on our journey, not to detain and entrap us. It saddens Him when we focus our attention on the mud puddles of life when He is offering us a vision of His glorious heaven.

We need to be like Abraham, who refused to trade mud puddles for oceans. When confronted by the allurements of this world, we're told that he rejected them because he was *"longing for a better country – a heavenly one."* As a result, *"God is not ashamed to be called* (his) *God, for he has prepared a city for* (him)." *(Heb. 11:16)* Even though Abraham was blessed with worldly goods, he was not content with temporary blessings, but *"was looking forward to the city with foundations, whose architect and builder is God." (Heb. 11:10)*

It takes faith to let go of that "mud puddle" in the hand in order to grab the "ocean" of God's future blessings. Without faith, *"it is impossible to please God, because anyone who comes to Him must believe that He exists and that the He rewards those who earnestly seek Him." (Heb. 11:6)* We hold onto the things of this world lightly, knowing they will never truly satisfy, and, by faith, we constantly reach out for God's glory, which is so much greater and more satisfying.

Mud puddles are fun, but they are temporary and they're not worth missing out on the glory that God has in store for all who long for Him. Isn't it time to quit playing in the mud puddles and start on the journey of finding God and His glory? The reward is worth it, so get started now.

Week 20

The Crossing

IN 1964 CONNER CREEK crossed the beach near Ocean City, Washington, and it was an obstacle in our path as we drove north on the wide, hard-packed sand beach. Jumping out of my 1947 Mercury, my high school buddies and I surveyed the creek crossing.

Conner Creek was shallow and not too wide, so we figured we could cross it safely. Still, the sight of a few rusting hulks half buried in the sand and water had us concerned, so we decided to not take any chances.

Picking a spot to cross, I backed the big Mercury up a hundred yards, shifted into first gear, gunned the flathead V8, popped the clutch and accelerated towards the creek. I was hunched over the steering wheel as my friends slapped the metal dash, urging our hulking metal monster to go faster.

We hit Conner Creek at fifty miles per hour!

Several things happened at that point. First, we almost went through the windshield! Second, we lost sight of the world as a wall of water enveloped our pea green marvel of speed. Third, the engine began to cough and sputter as if it were drowning, which it was. And fourth, we came to a complete stop just inches on the other side of Conner Creek. The Merc wasn't dead in the water, but it was dead!

Moments later we watched, with red faces, as an older gentleman slowly drove across the creek without hardly leaving a wake. After crossing Conner Creek, he was nice enough to give us a push and we were on our way again, wetter, but wiser.

Life is much like a crossing. Because of inexperience, or foolishness, many of us struggle getting to the other side. Sadly, some never make it. As Solomon warned us in Prov. 14:12, *"There is a way that seems right to a man, but in the end, it leads to death."*

Sometimes this truth is obvious. We recognize it in the joy ride accident, or the alcohol addiction, or the ruined marriage, or the wasted career, or a host of other wreckages. Sometimes, though, the damage isn't obvious and we hide our failures from others, but it is still real and painful. Often, we don't realize the losses we have endured in life because of our foolishness and refusal to change.

Whether we realize it or not though, the only crossing that really matters in life is the crossing at the end of our lives, when we cross over from this life to eternity. When we reach the other side, we'll find out if our life had value or not. We won't make this judgment ourselves because only God is the Judge. The Bible tells us: *"For we must all appear before the judgment seat of Christ, so that each may be repaid for what he has done in the body, whether good or evil." (2 Cor. 510)*

What will the standard of judgment be? It won't be our so-called good works, since *"there is no one righteous, not even one"* (Rom. 3:10) in God's eyes. The only standard that will be used is the one summed up in the Law, "You shall love the Lord your God with all your heart, soul, mind and strength" and *"You shall love your neighbor as yourself."* (Mt 22:37, 39) When we stand before Jesus, He will ask us, "Do you love Me?"

Many of us feel, yes, I love Jesus, but love is not a feeling; it's an action. If we love Jesus, our lives will demonstrate that love. We will love because He first loved us and His love will operate in our hearts and lives. Five times the Apostle John says, *"This is love for God, to obey His commands."* (1 Jn 5:3) If we really understood that Christ not only created us, but every moment sustains our lives, this would be an easy choice to make.

For those who love Jesus Christ, Solomon gives us good advice in Proverbs 3:5-6. *"Trust in the Lord with all your heart and lean not on our own understanding; in all your ways acknowledge Him and He will direct your paths."* If we will do this, we'll not only cross the shallow waters in life safely, but also the deep waters, and, eventually, the crossing into eternity.

May God bless you as you consider the crossings in life.

Week 21

The Marriage Go Round

THE CAPTION OF A MARRIAGE counseling cartoon read:

"When I got married
I was looking for an ideal-
Then it became an ordeal,
And now I want a new deal!"

If this wasn't the truth it would be funny. It is serious business, though, because lives and marriages are being destroyed through separations and divorces. Polls taken over thirty years ago showed that approximately fifty percent of all marriages ended in divorce; another thirty-five percent of marriages were considered unsatisfactory, but stayed together for various reasons (the kids, my folks, the church, I was taught to stick out, etc.); and another ten percent of marriages were considered satisfactory. That left just five percent of all marriages that were considered happy over an extended period of time. If these same polls were taken today, the result would probably be worse, not better.

Obviously, the American people are not very successful in this relationship that we call marriage. Now, with more and more people choosing living together without marriage, we are witnessing an unprecedented attack on marriage in our country.

Experts tells us that there are three major changes that are taking place in the institution of marriage:

1. A decline in understanding between marriage partners.
2. The loss of determination to stay married.
3. The development of unrealistic marriage expectations.

Obviously, if a marriage is to exist and flourish, couples need to turn each of these areas around. There must be an open, deep level of communication between partners if they are to learn to understand each other. There must be a deep level of commitment to making the marriage work, no matter what. There must be a mature, realistic expectation of what constitutes a good marriage. Basically, we need to change our attitudes toward marriage. Unfortunately, many people decide that it is easier to change partners than it is to change attitudes.

What must be done to promote a happy and successful marriage?

First, make adequate preparation for the marriage. Most people spend more time preparing for a driver's license than they do for a marriage. Take advantage of the hundreds of marriage manuals that are available to help you navigate the curves, bumps and pitfalls of marriage. All of us can learn from other people's successes and failures.

Second, commit yourself to making the marriage work, no matter what. Take seriously the vows you made before God that nothing but death will separate us. Realize that disappointments and hard times are bound to come, but with love, effort and prayer they can be worked through and overcome. The rewards are great for those who work through their problems.

Third, go to the One who created and designed marriage. It is God's purpose and desire that a marriage be fulfilling and exciting. When couples give themselves to God and let Him take control of their lives and marriages, then He makes something beautiful out of it. He helps us understand each other; He changes our attitudes; He channels new and better expectations.

"What if someone isn't meeting my needs," someone may ask. "Do I still have to stay with them?"

If someone asks this, it reveals that they have no comprehension of what real love is. Expecting someone to meet my needs isn't love – it is using them for my own selfish ends. Real love gives, even when it doesn't receive anything back for its sacrifice. We see many examples of sacrificial love when someone serves a partner who is unable to return that love in a physical way because of an accident or illness. Of course, the ultimate example of this kind of love is God, who gave His Son Jesus for us even when we were His enemies, unable to love Him because of our self-love. I believe that God is glorified when we love and serve our partner sacrificially.

The world's system for happiness, contentment and joy is not working – it is a pipe dream, an illusion. God's system for marriage has been tried and proven and it works. When marriage is centered on glorifying the God of Heaven, then it becomes the next best thing to heaven.

Week 22

Dealing with Diversity

LAST WEDNESDAY MY DAUGHTER Jenni walked into the room with a birthday balloon, gave me a big hug and wished me, "Happy birthday!" What could be better than your daughter taking a day off work and driving down from Carnation to celebrate your birthday with you? Well, as it turns out, a whole lot could have been better.

The day before, a Tuesday, I left my office to walk home for lunch. After walking up the hill to our house, I was completely out of breath and it took me almost ten minutes to recover. "Something's wrong," I thought, so I called Jenni, who is a nurse.

"It sounds like you may have congestive heart failure," she suggested. "I think you should go to the emergency room." When I hesitated, she scolded me, "This is serious, Dad, you need to have this looked at."

Sondra and I arrived at St. Peter's Hospital in Olympia at four p.m. and checked into the emergency room, where we were told to take a seat and wait for my name to be called. Fifteen minutes later someone called and I walked up to the front desk, where a young lady made sure my personal information was correct. Finished, she instructed me, "Okay, take a seat and wait for your name to be called." Then she added, "We're really busy tonight. It might be awhile."

Seven hours later, I had had two blood tests, two EKG's, an X-ray, an ultra sound on my legs, a CAT-scan on my chest and multiple exams by several doctors. Oh, and did I mention the waiting – in the lobby, in the initial exam room, in the emergency room hallway, and, finally, in an emergency exam room.

At first, they suspected a heart attack. One doctor told me, "Well, Mr. Richards, one of your blood enzymes is high - it looks like you've had a heart attack recently. We're probably going to admit you for further tests." Then he added, "If we can find you a room. The hospital is full."

When they found a blood clot in my right leg, they did admit me and I took a long wheelchair ride to the nearby Emilee Pavilion. After getting me settled in, I was taken to have the CAT-scan and they found the pulmonary embolism in my right lung. Back in my room, the doctor told me what they found and prescribed treatment of blood thinners for the next six months. He explained, "The blood thinner keeps you from having any more clots and the enzymes in your body will eventually dissolve the clot and embolism." He finished with, "Try to get some rest and we'll see how you are in the morning." By then, it was after midnight, so He added, "Happy birthday."

Did I say rest? They inserted an IV needle in my arm, hooked me up to an IV drip and an EKG monitor, took my blood pressure, gave me a blood thinner shot in my belly and, then, settled me in for the night. Even though I felt short of breath, I quickly fell asleep, which didn't last long. An hour later, and every hour after that, a nurse came into the room to take my blood pressure and check my vitals. Twice, an orderly came into the room and took blood for some more tests. I really only slept from six a.m. to eight a.m.

Needless to say, this wasn't what I was expecting for my birthday. The truth is, none of us know what the next day will bring. What we can know and what I experienced is that God *"will never leave you or forsake you."* (Heb. 13:15) When I was sitting on a gurney in the emergency room hallway and they still hadn't found out what was wrong with me, I had a tremendous peace in my heart. I was reminded of Isaiah's words, who said, *"You keep him in perfect peace whose mind is stayed on you, because he trusts in you." (Is. 26:3)* I didn't know what the outcome would be, but I knew that God was in control and that I could trust Him, whether He wanted to heal me or take me home to heaven. I was ready for either.

I thank God for the dedicated, competent and courteous staff at the hospital. Not only was my wife Sondra there to bless me, as well as my daughter, but God had scheduled Devin and Jane Backholm to be in the area that morning. We all had a great time praising God for His wonderful love for us. Most importantly, I knew that many were praying for my recovery and I felt the presence of God with me in the hospital. What a wonderful thing it is to be a part of a loving, caring Christian body. I know people depend on their families at times like this, which is a blessing, but a church family is a special blessing to all God's children.

So, I praise God for His goodness. Like the Apostle Paul, I was ready to die if that was His plan for my life, which would be far better than anything this world offers. If it was His will that I live, I dedicated myself to serve Him and Jesus with whatever strength and time He would give me. I truly believe that God gives good gifts to His children and I thank Him for the gift of life.

Week 23

Condition – Cause – Cure

RECENTLY I WENT TO the hospital for a **condition** that had a **cause** and needed a **cure**. My **condition** was shortness of breath, which was **caused** by a clot and a pulmonary embolism, and the **cure** required blood thinners for six months so my body can dissolve the blood clots.

Obviously, if our body is compromised, we want to see it restored. As important as our body health is, though, it pales in comparison to our spiritual health. Concerning our faith, Peter tells us our faith is "of greater worth than gold" (1 Peter 1:7) and is the most important thing we possess. Is it any wonder that our enemy, the Devil, wants to destroy our faith?

In his first letter to Timothy, twice Paul tells Timothy to "fight the good fight of faith." Paul shares **five conditions** where someone's faith has failed, reveals the **cause** in each case, and prescribes the **cure** needed to restore their faith. Since every Christian is in a battle to hold onto their faith, Paul's **condition, cause and cure** is vitally important to our spiritual health.

Condition #1 is faith that has been shipwrecked (1 Tim. 1:19). A ship wrecks when it goes off course and runs into the rocks, usually with great loss of life. Paul shares that among those who shipwrecked their faith were "Hymenaeus and Alexander". Paul states that the **cause** of their shipwreck was blasphemy. Blasphemy is attributing something about God that is not true. In this case they rejected the faith that had been handed down by the Apostles and did not hold onto a good conscience. Probably, they were saying things about God that did not come from the Scriptures and were leading others astray. Their condition was so serious that Paul prescribed a drastic remedy for their sin. In their case, the **cure** for their condition was handing them "over to Satan so they would learn not to blaspheme."

Condition #2 is faith that has been abandoned (1 Tim. 4:1). Some fell away, or gave up, or departed, from the original faith they had received. The **cause** of their departure was deception by "deceiving spirits and things taught by demons." Instead of focusing on spiritual truths that are taught in the Word of God, they listened to teachings about natural things like "abstaining from certain foods", thinking this would make them more spiritual. The **cure** in this case is to be "consecrated by the Word of God and prayer" and to "train yourself to be godly", which has value for both this life and the life to come.

Condition #3 is a faith that has been denied (1 Tim. 5:8). These folks didn't deny Christ by their words but by their actions. The **cause** of this denial was the failure to take care of their families. Paul accuses them of being "worse than unbelievers". The **cure** for their condition is "to put their religion into practice by caring for their own family." John echoes this truth by telling us to "not love with words or tongue but with actions and in truth."

Condition #4 is a faith that has been wandered away from (1 Tim. 6:10). It has the idea of straying or losing your footing, which isn't deliberate, but still results in "piercing themselves with many griefs." The **cause** of this condition is "the love of money, which is a root of all kinds of evil." Paul warns us that "people who want to get rich fall into temptation and a trap and into many foolish and harmful desires that plunge men into ruin and destruction." They wanted more, even when there was enough. The **cure** for this foolishness is realizing that "godliness with contentment is great gain". Paul commands the "people who are rich in this present world to do good, to be rich in good deeds and to be generous and willing to share." By taking this approach to material goods, it saves us many griefs.

Condition #5 is a faith that misses the mark (1 Tim. 6:21). Paul is warning Timothy about people who see religion as a grand contest. They get caught up in doctrines and methods, splitting hairs over obscure teachings and loving to debate. The **cause** of their condition is turning aside to "godless chatter and the opposing ideas of what is falsely called knowledge." They become proud of their knowledge and understanding and miss what really matters. The **cure** for this puffed up pride is to guard the basic truths that have been handed down to us through the Scriptures. It is realizing that hitting the mark is humbling ourselves in order to serve others.

If anyone was in danger of experiencing these **five conditions**, it was the Apostle Paul. He shared in 2 Cor. 12 that he was in danger of becoming conceited because of the great revelations God had given him. God protected him by giving him a "thorn in the flesh" to teach him that "God's grace is sufficient ... for My power is made perfect in weakness." God protect us from these conditions that erode our faith! Help us realize what causes these conditions and apply your cure to our souls.

Week 24

Pride Goes Before... Pneumonia!

ONE OF THE GREATEST follies in life is to think we're something when, in fact, we are nothing. Pride strips away our façade of self-exaltation and reveals our incomprehensible illusion of self-worship. Instead of acknowledging our complete dependence on God, pride causes us to believe that we have gifts that add value to our Creator. Pride calls Jesus, who said *"Apart from Me you can do nothing"* *(John 15:5)*, a liar and challenges God's Sovereignty over every aspect of our lives.

Because God is Holy, He cannot let our self-exaltation go unchecked since it would eventually lead to our complete and total destruction in Hell for all eternity. To save us from the consequences of our self-worship, God warns us over and over in Scripture that "pride goes before a fall", and He allows us to reap the consequences our pride, with the intent of saving us from our folly. I am learning this lesson in greater detail and depth and can add, sooner or later pride <u>always</u> goes before a fall. No exceptions!

As an example of this, I recently learned that pride goes before pneumonia. I'm not kidding! I was sitting in my daughter's hot tub on a Friday night visiting with my son-in-law about spiritual things when our conversation somehow, incomprehensibly, shifted to pneumonia. I had never had pneumonia, so in my mind, without even realizing it, I somehow considered myself an expert on pneumonia. So, I shared my story with my son-in-law.

Twenty-eight years ago, the county set up a shot clinic here at the church and I went with the intention of getting a flu shot. After signing in, the county nurse asked me, "Do you want a flu shot or a pneumonia shot?"

Unsure what to do and short of cash, I asked the nurse, "What's the difference in price?"

She answered, "The flu shot costs ten dollars and lasts a year and the pneumonia shot costs fifteen dollars and lasts the rest of your life." I'm not a math major, but even I could figure out that ten dollars a year versus fifteen dollars a lifetime is a no brainer.

After receiving the pneumonia shot, I began to notice that my colds were not as severe as they had been. Before, they dropped into my lungs and lasted weeks, where now they seemed less severe and usually lasted a few days. I began to sing the praises of pneumonia shots, using myself as an example of their miracle powers. Unfortunately, pride was just below the surface of my awareness, congratulating me for making such an amazing decision. The truth was, I was proud of my decision to get that pneumonia shot!

Now, back to Friday night. By Sunday afternoon, I began feeling a tightness in my chest, which I attributed to my lingering recovery from my pulmonary embolism (PE) in January. On Monday afternoon I coughed up some phlegm, so I fired up my sauna to help clear my chest. On Monday night I coughed violently all night, trying to clear my lungs of the mucus that was building up in them with no success. Tuesday morning, tired and exhausted and fearing there was a complication from my PE, I went to the emergency room in Olympia, where they X-rayed my chest.

The doctor said, "You have pneumonia in both lungs. We don't know if it is bacterial or viral, but I'm prescribing an anti-biotic, and you should be better in a few days."

Shocked, I protested, "How can that be? I have had the pneumonia shot!"

He explained, "There's many strains of pneumonia and the shot doesn't work against them all." Then he added, "You should be feeling better in a few days." Which I am!

Did I get pneumonia because I bragged to my son-in-law about getting the pneumonia shot? I don't know. What I do know is this: *"God opposes the proud but gives grace to the humble."* (Prov. 3:34, James 4:6; 1 Peter 5:5)

Whenever pride rears its ugly head in our lives, whether we realize it or not, we challenge God's sovereignty, wisdom and power. We proclaim that a small part of creation somehow has mastery over the Creator. When we do this, God's glory demands justice and submission. We can voluntarily submit to God now or we will be forced to submit when we stand before His Judgment throne. One way or another, we will all bow and *"confess that Jesus Christ is Lord, to the glory of God the Father."* (Phil. 2:11)

Humility is the currency of the Kingdom. Humility acknowledges our sin and asks God to save us; humility admits our weakness and cries out for grace to strengthen us; humility exposes our prejudice and begs for compassion; humility exalts God and allows Him to bless us.

"Humble yourselves, therefore, under God's mighty hand, that He may lift you up in due time. Cast all your anxiety on Him because He cares for you." (1 Pet. 5:6,7)

Week 25
Above All Else...

SOMETIMES THE PROBLEM is not the problem. I discovered this last week.

On Sunday, I told my wife Sondra, "If I don't sleep any better tonight, I'm going to the emergency room in the morning." I had been struggling for breath the past two weeks and was only sleeping three to five hours each night, and it was wearing me out.

On Monday, after a fitful night and three hours of sleep, we left early for Providence St. Peter in Olympia, arriving to an almost empty emergency room at 8 am. I checked in, saw a doctor, who ordered an X-ray and a C-scan to check my lungs. He reported that I still had some small clots from the pulmonary embolism I experienced four months earlier, but they were dissolving as expected.

"That's good," I thought, but then the doctor shocked me, "We're admitting you to check your heart."

On Tuesday I had an echo-cardiogram, which revealed that my heart function was fifteen. A normal heart pumps at 55-65 % efficiency, so my heart was operating at 25% of its normal rate. Shocked again!

On Wednesday I had an angiogram, where they run small cameras into your heart through your arteries. After the test the doctor told me, "Your heart arteries are clear and there is no heart muscle damage, so we don't know why your heart is so weak."

Good news? Not sure.

On Thursday and Friday, they administered drugs and monitored me. Finally, on Saturday, feeling much better, the hospital dismissed me. Sondra and I left for home with the goal of strengthening my heart. Driving home I was reminded of Proverbs 4:23, which says, *"Above all else, guard your heart, for it is the wellspring of life."* This is true physically and spiritually. If you have heart problems, you have life problems. There are regimens to help our physical hearts, but what about our spiritual hearts?

The Bible is clear that our spiritual hearts are sick. Just before the flood, *"The Lord saw how great man's wickedness had become, and that every inclination of the thoughts his heart was only evil all the time." (Gen. 6:5)* Centuries later, Jeremiah confirmed God's initial assessment of our hearts when he said, *"The heart is deceitful above all things and beyond cure. Who can understand it?" (Jer. 17:9)*

The heart is beyond cure and there is nothing we can do to change it or save it from sin. The truth is, we are all in a desperate need of a heart transplant. That's why God promised, *"I will give them an undivided heart and put a new spirit in them; I will remove from them their heart of stone and give them a heart of flesh."* When we receive this new heart God promises, *"Then they will follow my decrees and be careful to keep my laws. They will be my people and I will be their God." (Ezekiel 11:19-20)*

Now, when someone is converted and born again, God gives them a new heart that loves Jesus Christ and desires to please Him. There will be a new hunger and thirst for righteousness and we will rejoice in what the Lord is doing in our lives. God's Word will refresh our souls and we will love our brothers and sisters in Christ. In short, there will be new life!

We might ask, though, what if my heart seems sluggish and unresponsive? What if I'm experiencing spiritual heart disease? Well, God has a prescription plan for your heart! In the Parable of the Sower in Luke 8:5-8, Jesus describes four kinds of hearts. He mentions the hard heart, the shallow heart, the worldly heart and the good heart. In Luke 8:15, He describes the good heart. *"But the seed* (the Word of God) *on the good soil stands for those with a noble and good heart, who hear the word, retain it, and by persevering produce a crop."*

Jesus reveals that there are three things we need to do to keep our spiritual hearts healthy.

First, we need to hear the Word. This means we listen to it and read it.

Second, we need to retain the Word. This means we need to reflect and meditate on the Word we are hearing and reading.

Third, we need to persevere. This is something we do for a lifetime, not weeks or months or even years. The goal is to produce a crop, which is spiritual fruit. If we do this, we will stay healthy spiritually and have a good heart.

I woke up Saturday morning in the hospital, turned to my daily Psalm reading, which said, *"My heart is steadfast, O God; I will sing and make music with all my soul."* (Ps 108:1) Amen!

Week 26

Huckleberry Heaven

HUCKLEBERRIES! IN pies, over ice cream, on pancakes, you name it, our family loved them. We were living in north central Idaho and we heard that the huckleberries were ripe in the mountains, so we rounded up the kids and the camping gear and took off for the Gospel Hump Wilderness area above Grangeville, Idaho.

We camped at picture perfect Rocky Bluff on Slate Creek. The kids played in the creek while camp was set up and we explored the old gold mining town of Florence after our campfire dinner. It had been a relaxing day, but we knew that, come morning, we would be all business as we searched for our little patch of huckleberry heaven.

We picked around Slate Creek in the morning. The area was beautiful, with plenty of huckleberry bushes, but the berries were few and far between. It seemed at times that we did more looking than picking. The kids became more and more discouraged as there were less and less berries. By noon we were somewhat disappointed since all we had to show for our efforts was one gallon of berries.

After lunch we broke camp and headed home, keeping a sharp eye out for a good berry patch somewhere alongside the road. It wasn't long before we spotted a likely place (sorry, I'm not telling where!) and we stopped to investigate. Eureka! We found them. The berries were so thick on the bushes that we picked three gallons in a couple of hours and didn't move more than thirty yards in the process. We were tired, dirty, stained, but we found what we were looking for – huckleberries! We felt satisfied as we drove home with our purple treasure.

The trip was nice, the scenery was beautiful, the huckleberry bushes were plentiful, but it was fruit we were looking for. Did you know that in the same way Christ is looking for fruit in our lives? All of the externals, no matter how nice or beautiful they may appear, don't matter if there is no fruit for the Master.

Jesus told a parable in Luke 13:6-9 to illustrate this truth:

> *"A man had a fig tree, planted in his vineyard, and he went to look for fruit on it, but did not find any. So, he said to the man who took care of the vineyard, 'For three years now I've been coming to look for fruit on this fig tree and haven't found any. Cut it down! Why should it use up the soil?' 'Sir,' the man replied, 'leave it alone for one more year, and I'll dig around it and fertilize it. If it bears fruit next year, fine! If not, then cut it down.'"*

Jesus told His disciples and us in John 15, *"I am the true vine and you are the branches. Every branch in me that does not produce fruit he removes, and he prunes every branch that produces fruit so that it will produce more fruit."* Later in that chapter, Jesus revealed the purpose for bearing fruit: *"My Father is glorified by this: that you produce much fruit and prove to be my disciples."*

Finally, Jesus shares how we can bear fruit: *"You did not choose me, but I chose you. I appointed you to go and produce fruit and that your fruit should remain, so that whatever you ask the Father in my Name, He will give you."* He sums up this teaching on bearing fruit by saying: *"This is what I command you: Love one another."*

Is there any fruit in your life for the Master? You may appear beautiful (leaves) and seem strong (branches), but without fruit you are in danger of being cut down and thrown into the fire. You were created to bear fruit for your Master and without it your life is meaningless.

Even now Christ wants to fertilize your life and prune away the dead branches so you can bear fruit. Won't you submit to Him and Allow Him to His work in you? If we love Jesus, nothing is so thrilling and fulfilling as producing fruit for the One who loved us and gave Himself.

Week 27

Two Lifetimes

I WAS STANDING IN FRONT of our church parsonage in Rosebud, Montana, when a local, older rancher pulled up in his pickup. He rolled his window down and asked, "Do you want to go with me to the auction in Miles City?"

"Sure!" I cried. "I'd love to see a cattle auction." I circled around the pickup, hopped in the passenger seat, and we headed east on I-94 to Miles City.

The rancher was in a talkative mood and started sharing stories about ranching in Eastern Montana, where the elements made ranching tough. There were the obvious long, hard winters, but summers were what often made conditions nearly impossible. If the drought didn't get you, the hail would, and if you survived both of those, nature would throw in a grasshopper plague or two to test your mettle. This man not only survived, but actually thrived under these harsh conditions.

Before we reached Miles City, the rancher turned philosophical. "You know," he mused, "a man needs two life times – one to learn everything and another to put it all into practice."

Unwittingly, this good man hit the one big problem with making anything in this life your hope or dream – eventually you lose it all. If all we hope and dream for are in this life, then we are to be pitied above all men because death will sooner or later separate us from everything we lived for.

Jesus exposes the folly of only living for this life by telling a story about a rich land owner in Luke 12:16. When the rich man had a bountiful crop and no place to store it, he said, *"This is what I'll do. I'll tear down my barns and build bigger ones, and there I'll store all my grain and my goods. And I'll say to myself, 'You have plenty of good things laid up for many years. Take life easy, eat, drink and be merry.'"*

This seemed like a good plan for the rich man until Jesus exposed his folly. *"But God said to him, 'You fool! This very night your life will be demanded from you. Then who will get what you have prepared for yourself?'"*

Then Jesus fires a warning shot across the bow of our lives. *"That's how it is with the one who stores up treasure for himself and is not rich toward God."* (Lk 12:21)

Many people ignore the future, as if that will keep them from facing it. Time marches on, though, whether we want to face it or not. Sooner or later we will all stand before Jesus Christ and give an account of our lives. Those who lived for Christ will inherit eternal life and those who lived for self will forfeit everything.

Jesus asked His disciples and us a probing question in Mark 8:36: *"What good is it for a man to gain the whole world, yet forfeit his soul?"* If my rancher friend had understood this, he would have realized that we do have an opportunity to live two lifetimes, but the second one is only found in Jesus Christ. (He did receive Jesus as his Savior before he died)

Paul's advice to his young protege Timothy applies to us all: *"Command those who are rich in this present world not to be arrogant nor to put their hope in wealth, which is so uncertain, but to put their hope in God, who richly provides us with everything for our enjoyment."* (1 Tim. 6:7)

Where is your hope today? If it is in anything other than Jesus Christ, it will fail you; if it is in Christ you can never fail.

Week 28

Keep Yourself from Idols

WE'VE ENJOYED A SHORT respite from the rain with some welcome sunshine, which is a subtle reminder that Spring is just around the corner. Ah ... Spring, which brings May flowers, baseball, long walks, gardens, picnics and ..., wait for it, ... and motorcycles! Yes, that's right, riding motorcycles!

Many years ago, my neighbor put his 850 Yamaha up for sale and I started dreaming and scheming, maybe even salivating, on how I could get my hands on that fine piece of equipment. I had no cash or savings, but I did receive $75 a month from some property I'd sold, so I went to my neighbor with a proposal that I hoped he couldn't resist. Like a dog begging for food, I approached my neighbor and offered, "I'll give you $75 a month for the next year if you'll sell me your bike." I'm not sure what I expected, but I certainly didn't expect to see the disdain in his eyes as he unceremoniously rejected my offer.

Dejected and crushed, I was walking back to my home when the Lord spoke to me. "You would have done almost anything for that motorcycle, wouldn't you? "I couldn't lie and admitted that what He said was true. Then God blindsided me, "I wonder what you would give for Me?" Ouch!

My heart was broken as I realized that I had coveted something more than Him. With tears in my eyes, I told God, "You are worth more than all of the motorcycles in the world to me." Then I made a commitment to Him, "Lord, I'm going to give that $75 a month to You." All of a sudden, the emptiness in my heart dissipated, like a morning fog, and I felt the presence of His joy, like a ray of sunshine peeking through the clouds. With gladness in my heart I gave that extra $75 to the Lord. When the property payment stopped a year later, I continued giving the extra $75, which is now going on 37 years. It is one of the best investments I have ever made.

The Apostle John finishes his first letter with these surprising words – *"Dear children, keep yourselves from idols."* (1 John 5:21) Many scholars believe that these words are not only the last words written in this letter, but the last words written in the Bible. Just like a last will and testament, the last words of a man like John are words that we need to pay attention to.

John began this letter by revealing God's purpose for us. He said, *"We proclaim to you what we have seen and heard, so that you also may have fellowship with us. And our fellowship is with the Father and with his Son, Jesus Christ."* (1 John 1:3) Fellowship in this case means a strong love for another person, where you want to share your life with them. Our first father Adam forfeited that fellowship when he sinned in the Garden, but Jesus Christ came to restore our relationship with God by dying in our place, paying our penalty, and making it possible to come back to God by faith. When we give our hearts to Jesus, we are admitting our need of oneness with Him; we are saying we want to have a relationship with God.

While the non-Christian does not and cannot have this relationship with God because of sin, the Christian struggles in his or her relationship with God for the same reason - sin. Idolatry puts the creation before the Creator. It looks for something, anything, in creation to provide our needs rather than looking to the Creator to meet them. Not wanting God to be God in our lives, we look for diversions and distractions that seemingly meet our needs, but they quickly become rabbit trails that lead nowhere. Sooner or later, everything that we pursue in creation fails us and leaves us panting for the true God, who alone can meet the needs of our hearts, which is a deep relationship with Him. We were created to have a relationship with God.

If God is not first in our lives, we quickly become like the Israelites in Judges, *"who did what was right in their own eyes."* (Jdg. 21:25) Even though it seemed right, it always led to slavery and destruction. In the same way, our idols, whether religion, family, friends, things, experiences or life itself, always fail us, eventually enslaving us and leaving us unfulfilled. If we are seeking anything more than God we are on a "fool's errand", thinking we can get something from nothing. If we do this as Christians everything in our lives will be burned up at the last Judgment and we will have nothing to give to God.

After Paul came to Christ, he realized the futility of seeking the things of this world instead of a deeper relationship with Jesus Christ. He said, *"What is more, I consider everything a loss compared to the surpassing greatness of knowing Christ Jesus my Lord, for whose sake I have lost all things."* (Phil. 3:8) He declared, *"I want to know Christ and the power of his resurrection and the fellowship of sharing in his sufferings, becoming like him in His death, and so, somehow, to attain to the resurrection from the dead."* May God deliver us from our idols and reveal to us the glory of Jesus, satisfying our hearts.

Week 29

Choose Your Destination Wisely

"HOW MUCH LONGER?" THE kids moaned from the backseat, their patience evaporating in the sweltering heat of the high Nevada desert.

"Not far, now," I reassured them. Still, they almost mutinied on me when we drove through the desert oasis of Winnemucca, with its motels and swimming pools beckoning us to stop and cool ourselves off.

We were traveling from Idaho to California to attend a Bible Conference and, unable to afford a motel room, I booked a reservation at the Rye Patch Reservoir Campground, which was halfway between Winnemucca and Reno in Nevada.

When we finally arrived at the Rye Patch Reservoir Campground, my wife looked at me incredulously and asked, "We drove five hundred miles for this?!"

Standing on shaky ground, I kept quiet. After all, it's hard to stick up for a paved campground filled with campers and motorhomes. I backed into an empty spot and started setting up the tent while everyone else looked around. My wife came back complaining about the lack of running water to clean up with and the kids were discouraged by the deep mud around the half empty reservoir. The brown, vegetation-less hills surrounding the campground depressed us even more.

"Well, maybe I can cheer everyone up with dinner," I thought, but no one liked what I made. Looking for a reprieve from the depressing campground, I waited anxiously for bedtime to arrive. When it finally did, we snuggled into our sleeping bags, hoping for a good night's sleep under the bright canopy of stars overhead. Unfortunately, sleep didn't seem to be on anyone else's agenda that night, with loud parties going on all around us far into the night.

We woke up the next morning tired and grumpy, silently packed up our camping equipment and headed for Lake Tahoe, where, hopefully, we would have a better camping experience (we did).

Most of us have experienced the frustration of reaching a destination that failed to live up to expectations. When I arrived, I wondered what could have possessed me to choose that particular spot. Whether we claim ignorance, or bad luck, or failing to plan, nothing changes the disastrous consequences of reaching a bad destination. As bad as this can be in life, it pales in comparison to our eternal destination.

God clearly states that there are two destinations in life. One, hell, is easy to find and many go there. The other, heaven, is hard to find and few go there. Our destination is determined by which path we've chosen in this life, either self or Christ.

Where is your destination? Philippians 3:18-21 helps us find out. Paul says, *"For, as I have often told you before and now say again even with tears, many live as enemies of the cross of Christ. Their destiny is destruction, their god is their stomach, and their glory is in their shame. Their mind is on earthly things."* The mind that is consumed by earthly things is headed to hell, a terrible destination that lasts for eternity.

On the other hand, Paul states, *"but our citizenship is in heaven. And we eagerly await a Savior from there, the Lord Jesus Christ, who by the power that enables Him to bring everything under His control, will transform our lowly bodies so that they will be like His glorious body."* (Phil. 3:20, 21) Christ is the key to our destiny. By dying in our place on the cross, He opened the door for us to come back to Father. Jesus is the entrance to eternal life and no one comes to the Father except through Him.

When my kids asked, "How much longer?", I answered, "Not far now." The truth is, all of us are on this short journey called life, and it won't be long until we arrive at our eternal destination. Thankfully, as long as it is still called "Today" you can choose your destination. Choose life, choose Christ.

For those of us who are headed to heaven, do everything you can to prepare yourself for spending eternity with your Savior. He loves you and is 'preparing a place' for you, so that you can with Him forever. Whether the journey is pleasant or difficult, keep your eyes on Jesus Christ, our destination - it is worth it!

Week 30

Life's Outhouses

OUR CABIN ON THE BEACH didn't have electricity, running water or any of the other amenities of modern life, but it did have an outhouse! Our third son, 9-month-old Jeremy, became curious about this little house that everyone visited so often and regularly, so one day he decided to investigate it. He waited for just the right moment, when mama was busy in the kitchen and not watching, and quickly crawled out the open front door to the path that led to the outhouse.

As luck would have it, the outhouse had no door to bar his entrance, so he crawled in, climbed up onto the seat, and gazed down into the dark hole. He only meant to look, but being unsteady, he lost his balance and fell through the hole into the dark abyss below.

It wasn't long before mama missed him and began searching. Not finding him in the cabin, she went outside and heard Jeremy's faint cries in the direction of the outhouse. Fearing the worst, she ran to the outhouse, heard Jeremy's cries from the bowels of the earth and looked down the hole to see her precious son crying and reaching out to be saved.

Oh, the despair and anguish as she reached as far as she could through the hole to rescue her young adventurer, who was just beyond her reach. She rushed back into the cabin, found a hammer and quickly returned to pry the outhouse seat off, allowing her to reach Jeremy's smelly and grimy hand. Somehow, Jeremy had landed on his hands and knees and was unharmed, although a little smellier for the experience.

He was a little worse for the wear, but he was at last safe in the arms of his mother, who would soon get him cleaned up again.

Through curiosity, overconfidence, or plain rebellion, people all around us are falling into life's outhouses. They become soiled and smelly and, often, can't free themselves from the trap they have fallen into. Their despair and anguish break the hearts of many who want to help, but are unable to.

The traps are numerous. Many stare into the abyss of alcohol or drugs. They are lured closer by the promise of fun and excitement until, finally, they fall in, unable to escape. Many are caught in the trap of sex. Looking for love and fulfillment, they enter into relationships outside of marriage, ignoring God's clear warning of judgment and destruction. The guilt and grief that results staggers the mind and breaks the heart of those who desire to help, but can't.

Satan has many other traps, which he baits with the allurement of our own self-satisfaction. Why do people fall for the bait? Paul tells us why in Philippians 3:19 when he says, *"Their mind is on earthly things."* Earthly things are temporary and can never satisfy the true needs of the heart.

The truth is, we were all made by God and for God. He alone can satisfy the true needs of our hearts. Jesus said, *"I have come that they may have life, and have it to the full."* (John 10:10) He not only wants to keep us out of life's outhouses, but He is ready and willing to rescue us if we have fallen into one. If we will cry out to Him, He is more than ready to reach down, grab our hand and pull us to safety. Sadly, very few turn to God for salvation and deliverance He offers them through Jesus Christ.

One man who did turn to God was Bill. His mother died when he was young and he was put in a Catholic orphanage. When he turned eighteen, he charged into the world searching for pleasure and fun. Twenty years later, after addictions, prison, and a failing marriage brought destruction into his life, he surrendered to Jesus Christ, who changed him from the inside out. After he was saved, he came by my house one Saturday morning for coffee and told me, "For thirty-nine years I did my best to have fun, but I didn't even know what fun was until I gave my life to Christ."

Bill went on to become a great husband, father and provider. When he passed into the presence of the Lord after dying from cancer eight years later, he had the joy of the Lord and the assurance of salvation in his heart.

How can we escape life's outhouses? It is no secret. David tells us in Psalm 119:105, *"Your Word is a lamp to my feet and light for my path."* When we commit our ways to Him and follow His Word, He directs our paths and keeps us from the pitfalls of life. He alone knows the path of life that will fulfill our souls.

It may be that you are trapped right now in one of life's outhouses and can't seem to escape. If so, cry out to the Lord for deliverance and cleansing. 1 John 1:9 promises that *"If we confess our sins, He is faithful and just, and will forgive us our sins and purify us from all unrighteousness."*

Turn to the Lord today for deliverance.

Week 31

The Fly in the Ointment

MY MOTHER WAS PROUD of her chili. So, after breakfast, she announced to my brother and I and our ten friends who were seated around our ocean cabin kitchen table, "Tonight we are going to have my famous chili for dinner!"

There was a quick round of applause, but it quickly died out when one of my Junior High friends pouted, "I don't like chili, and I'm not going to eat it."

"Just try it and you'll like it," my mother challenged him. Then she added, "Even chili haters like my chili." Her confidence would have evaporated if she had noticed the gleam of defiance in my friend's eyes.

After breakfast we walked down the beach to nearby Ocean Shores and spent the day exploring while my mother lovingly cooked the chili beans on the cabin's wood cook range. When the beans were soft enough, she added her special chili recipe and let it simmer the rest of the day, filling the cabin with a delightful chili aroma.

All of us, except my chili hating friend, were hungry for chili that night. My mother tried coaxing my friend into trying the chili, but he wouldn't budge. He just sat there and watched us kind of strange as we all gorged ourselves on chili and corn bread. If we had been more attentive, we might have recognized our danger and skipped the meal, but we ate away.

It wasn't long, though, until, one by one, all of us chili eaters got this funny look on our faces and a queasy feeling in our stomachs and, then, made a mad dash to the cabin's outhouse. As I stood there in line with my stomach churning, my only thought was, "We should have built a two-holer instead of a one-holer!" Meanwhile, my mother kept apologizing, "My chili never did this before!" but that didn't change matters at all.

It was years later, after the statute of limitations had passed, that I learned that it wasn't the chili that was at fault, but the box of Ex-Lax that my friend had dumped into the chili when no one was looking. We had all been living testimonials to Ex-Lax's effectiveness. I can truthfully say, a little bit of it goes a long way.

Another thing that goes a long way is our tongue. It is such a small member of our body and, yet, it often does great damage to others. A careless word, a spiteful accusation, a little gossip here and there and people's lives are affected, sometimes irrevocably.

As James says,

> *"Likewise, the tongue is a small part of the body, but it makes great boasts. Consider what a great forest is set on fire by a small spark. The tongue also is a fire, a world of evil among the parts of the body. It corrupts the whole person, sets the whole course of his life on fire, and it itself set on fire by hell." (James 3:5-6)*

What my friend did to my mother's chili that day was a dirty trick, but it was trivial compared to what some people say about others. Gossip is one of the worst of sins and we should do everything in our power to stop it, including not listening to it. Let's say, "Brothers, this should not be."

Week 32

Where Worms Don't Die

I LOVE SPRING! DAYS get longer, the sun warms the earth, plants and trees leaf and flower, grass grows, birds return and ... I get to work in my garden!

I've learned a lot of things gardening. For example, your seed seldom sprouts if you don't prepare the soil first. Then, you constantly fight the weeds to keep them from choking out the good seed. Also, you develop patience waiting for your fruit and vegetables to mature before you pick them. There's lots of good analogies about life you can learn from gardening.

Another thing I've learned from gardening is that worms don't have it so good. Worms? Yes, worms! For example, when I spade the soil, I often cut worms in half. Slice! Oh, don't forget the Robins, who love worms. They search my garden for any stray worms that get too close to the surface. Gulp! Then there are the boys looking for worms to use as bait for fishing. Being on a hook waiting for a fish to eat you can't be pleasant. As my daughter used to say, "Ugh!" I think the worst, in my opinion, are the rainy days that drive the worms out of the soil onto the roads. Their spineless bodies are no match for cars. Smash!

Fortunately for worms, though, is that when it is over, it's over. The slice, gulp, ugh and smash take place in a moment of time and then it's over, finished. As unpleasant as the worm's demise was, it ended.

There is a place, though, where the pain never ends. In a discourse on Hell Jesus described the unending agony by saying, "where their worm does not die, and the fire is not quenched." (Mark 9:48) Jesus is saying that there will be no end to the torment of Hell – you don't die, the fire doesn't go out, there is no end to the suffering.

We don't like to think about Hell, but Jesus talked about Hell more than anyone else. Why? Because He doesn't want anyone to go there! He is fully aware of how terrible Hell is – He experienced it for three hours on the cross when He became sin for you and I - and He warns us of the danger of going there. Speaking about Hell, the writer to the Hebrews warns us, *"It is a dreadful thing to fall into the hands of the living God." (Heb. 10:31)*

We have a lot of misconceptions about Hell. Many believe that God is a God of love, so He would never send someone to Hell. They neglect God's Holiness, which demands justice for all who reject Christ and remain in sin.

Some think that Hell won't be that bad, since "all my friends will be there." It's true that Hell will be overpopulated, but Hell is also a place of utter darkness and solitude, where people suffer alone. There is no solace in Hell.

Many don't believe in Hell. Their mantra is, "when it's over it's over!" They embrace annihilation, forgetting we are made in the image of God, which means we will live forever, either with God in Heaven, or without God in Hell. Annihilation is wishful thinking!

Some religions teach that we get a second chance after we die. Essentially, they offer people an excuse to "live like Hell" now, and pay for it later in Purgatory, or limbo, or wherever. They mock Jesus' payment for our sin on the Cross and foolishly believe they can make their own payment for sin.

The real issue for all of us is: where will you spend eternity? Are you headed for everlasting torment where "their worm does not die"; or are you headed for everlasting joy where *"our Lord God Almighty reigns"* (Rev. 19:6)? If you reject Jesus' offer of salvation through His blood and sacrifice, there is nothing left *"but a fearful expectation of judgment and of raging fire." (Heb. 10:27)*

If, on the other hand, you have chosen to make Jesus Christ your Lord and Savior and are following Him, He says *"I will come back and take you to be where I am."* (Jn. 14:3) You will have the double blessing of walking with Christ in this life and spending eternity with Him in the next life. The Apostle Paul shares *"that no eye has seen, no ear has heard, what God has prepared for those who love Him – but god has revealed it to us by His Spirit." (1 Cor. 2:9)*

The next time you see a worm, ask yourself, "Where am I going to spend eternity?" Jesus loves you and wants you to spend eternity with Him.

Week 33

On the Rocks

SURPRISED BY A SUDDEN Pacific Northwest storm, the Westport, Washington, fishing fleet scurried back to the safety of their port in Grays Harbor. A gale wind, with fog, driving rain and 30' waves, made the bar crossing at the mouth of Grays Harbor a perilous experience for even seasoned pilots.

With fog horns blaring on both sides of the harbor, my cousin Ted was piloting his forty-eight-foot trawler over the harbor bar when he heard a cry for help on his radio. "Mayday, Mayday! Our engine is out and we're drifting towards the rocks on the South Jetty." The desperation in the caller's voice was obvious and it was clear that he was in an extremely dangerous situation.

Through years of experience Ted recognized the floundering boat's position and quickly changed course. Even though the visibility was near zero and he would be putting himself in a hazardous position, he still felt a responsibility to help rescue the drifting boat. He knew the Coast Guard couldn't get there in time to save the crew.

Groping through the fog while listening to the plea for help over his radio, Ted heard the crashing of the waves on the rock jetty. Wary, he peered into what seemed like pea soup, when he finally caught sight of the disabled boat, which was only yards from the rocks and certain death. He swung his boat around and threw a lifeline to the anxious pilot on the disabled boat. As soon as the line was secured, Ted started pulling him away from the jetty rocks, only minutes before the boat would have been dashed to pieces.

Safe at last, the Coast Guard arrived on the scene and towed the disabled boat back into the calm waters of the Westport marina. Because of my cousin Ted's quick response, the crew of the other boat were alive to fish another day.

One of the greatest dangers the Christian faces is the danger of drifting away from his or her secure position in the Lord. Often it is because we are not paying attention to the spiritual dangers around us and we drift dangerously close to temptations that threaten to destroy our faith.

When you're "on the rocks," powerless to save yourself, who do you look to for help? God says that if we love Him, He will deliver us. *"Because he loves me,"* says the Lord, *"I will rescue him; I will protect him, for he acknowledges my Name. He will call upon Me, and I will answer him; I will be with him in trouble, I will deliver him and honor him." (Psalm 93:14, 15)*

King David often found himself in perilous situations, when it seemed that the storms of life would destroy him on the rocks of adversity. At such times he would cry out, *"Reach down your hand from on high; deliver me and rescue me from the mighty waters." (Psalm 144:7)* Over and over, David was able to testify, *"I sought the Lord, and He answered me; He delivered me from all my fears. The angel of the Lord encamps around those who fear Him, and He delivers them." (Psalm 34:4,7)*

We live in dangerous times, so it is important that we pay close attention to what God is telling us in His Word. Many of our problems would simply disappear if we would only heed God's Word and do what it says. Psalm 119:1-2 tells us, *"How happy are those whose way is blameless, who walk according to the Lord's instruction! Happy are those who keep His decrees and seek Him with all their heart."* When we pay close attention to what God has revealed to us in His Word, we can safely navigate through the troubled waters of life around us.

If we find ourselves drifting and floundering in a sea of adversity, we can call upon the Lord to rescue us. Whether we are on the rocks because of our own carelessness or foolishness or just blown off course by the stiff headwinds of life, God invites us to *"call upon Me in the day of trouble; and I will rescue you, and you will honor Me." (Psalm 50:15).* The Psalmist says,

> *"I love the Lord because He has heard my appeal for mercy. Because He has turned His ear to me, I will call out to Him as long as I live. The ropes of death were wrapped around me and the torments of Sheol overcame me; I encountered trouble and sorrow. Then I called on the Name of Lord, "Lord, save me!" The Lord is gracious and righteous; our God is compassionate. The Lord guards the inexperienced; I was helpless, and He saved me." (Psalm 116:1-6)*

What God has done for others He can do for you. Call upon the Lord today!

Week 34

When Fears Arise

ONE OF THE WORST FEARS a father can face is the possible loss of a child. I faced that possibility as I stood behind our parsonage in Rosebud, Montana, scanning the Yellowstone River in flood stage. I thought to myself, "No one could survive if they fell into those angry waters." Our three-year-old son Jeremy was missing and I was afraid that he might have accidentally fallen into the river.

Earlier that day our three boys, (six-year-old Justin, five-year-old John and three-year-old Jeremy), asked if they could go to the little store in Rosebud (population 200) to get a candy bar. It was okay with us, so we told them to walk up the dry Butte Creek bed (we had done this many times together) that ran beside our parsonage so they wouldn't have to cross the railroad tracks or highway. Our last words were, "Be careful and stay together."

A little later, we heard the kids playing outside in the yard, so we assumed that they were home safe. When the two older boys walked in the door, we asked, "Where's Jeremy?"

They answered, "We don't know - we haven't seen him for ten minutes," and I immediately thought about the swollen Yellowstone River behind our home. If Jeremy kept going down the dry creek bed he would have come to the river.

I ran out the door and into the creek bed, hollering, "Jeremy! Jeremy!" stopping to listen for a reply. Nothing but silence. I rushed down the creek and was confronted by the angry, boiling Yellowstone and a sickening feeling rose in my stomach as I realized that Jeremy could be in those churning waters.

Searching for alternatives, I ran to the nearby school yard, hoping that he might be playing there. He wasn't. Filled with a deepening fear and despair, I walked back toward home, pondering the possibility of life without Jeremy.

Just then a verse popped into my mind: *"And we know that in all things God works for the good of those who love Him, who have been called according to His purpose." (Romans 8:28)*

Suddenly, a peace flooded over me as I accepted this truth. God loves me and He loves Jeremy, I reasoned, so nothing can happen to either one of us that isn't for our good. Silently, I committed Jeremy's care and well-being to his Heavenly Father and continued walking home, secure in God's love.

We found Jeremy soon after that. Confused, he got turned around and went up the creek instead of down it. I found him crying about 100 yards up the creek from our home. For him, it was just another trying day in the life of a toddler. For me, it was a day where I turned my children over to the Lord and found His peace "which transcends all understanding."

Possibly you are experiencing difficulties in some area of your life. Now is a good time to go to God and put your trust in His sovereign care for you. Tell Him you love Him and you know He loves you and you are trusting Him to accomplish His purposes in your life. If you will do this, you, too, can experience God's peace in your life no matter what situation you may find yourself.

Week 35
Strength for Today

CONCERN FOR THE FUTURE often consumes the strength we contain for today. A desire to own a home dramatically demonstrated this to me many years ago.

"There goes another $275," I complained to my wife as I wrote out the rent check. "The only way we'll ever get ahead is to own a house," I concluded with a sudden flash of inspiration. It seemed like an innocent beginning, but it proved an exhaustive and expensive ordeal over the next year.

First, I found an older home on a 5-acre plot that seemed in our price zone. I borrowed $800 from my grandmother for a down payment and notified our landlord that we would be moving out of our apartment the end of the month. I can't remember how it happened, but the deal fell through and we lost our $800. Then, to add insult to injury, when I told our landlord that we weren't moving after all, he informed me that he had already rented our apartment to someone else, but we could move into another one of his apartments, just like the one we were already in, that he owned across town. Talk about frustration!

Later I heard about someone who would let us live in a house rent free if we would do some work on the side. I got up two hours early every morning to move sprinkler pipe in his alfalfa field and came home exhausted after work to a half-finished house that I had no idea how to fix it. On top of that, the house was surrounded by a beet field!

When the wind blew, dust would seep into the house and my oldest son developed asthma. Another disaster!

One day, frustrated by my efforts to own a home, I admitted to the Lord that my desire for independence and self-security had gotten me nowhere. In prayer I confessed, "Lord, if you want us to rent the rest of our lives, that's okay with me. I know I can trust you to meet all of our needs." I arose from prayer with a new sense of peace and contentment and put the desire to own a home of our own behind me.

Weeks later I noticed a "house for sale" sign on our bulletin board at work. I asked someone where the house was located and they said, "It's just over the bank from the parking lot."

I walked outside, looked over at the bank and there was the same house that was advertised on the bulletin board. Later that week, after church, I asked an older man if he would look at the house with me. He agreed and we set up a time to look at the house.

After looking at the house, we went outside and he asked me, "Are you interested in this house?"

I replied, "Yes," and then added, "but I don't have any money saved up."

Then he asked, "How much do they want for the house?"

I answered, "$16,500."

"Offer them $10,000," he stated matter-of-factly. When I reminded him, "But I don't have any money," he added, "If they accept our offer I'll loan you the money and we'll set up a contract for you to pay me back."

To make a long story short, they accepted our offer and we bought the house for $10,000. Nine months later I was hired by Ocean Spray Cranberries and we moved to my grandmother's cabin near Ocean City, where we started attending Copalis Community Church. We sold our house for $17,500 and when I felt called to go into the ministry, the money we made from selling the house helped pay for my Bible School tuition. God had been taking care of my needs all along and I simply needed to wait on Him. He took care of my needs as I needed them, not as I worried about them.

Concerning tomorrow's worries, Christ counsels us, *"therefore do not worry about tomorrow, for tomorrow will worry about itself. Each day has enough trouble of its own." (Matthew 6:34)*

When we trust Jesus Christ with our lives, He takes care of us today and every day of our lives. Let's pray that we will learn this lesson and pray the way He taught us, "Give us today our daily bread."

Week 36

Beating Bitterness

IF YOU HAPPENED TO read the Book (the *Bible*) or saw the movie (*The Ten Commandments*, Paramount Pictures, 1956), then you probably know what happened when Israel was hemmed in by Pharaoh and the Egyptian Army at the Red Sea. With the Red Sea in front of them and the Egyptians behind them, Moses cried out to God and He parted the sea, allowing Israel to cross the sea unharmed and drowning the Egyptian Army that pursued them.

Do you know what happened immediately after that, though?

Exodus 15:22-27 tells us that Israel left the Red Sea and traveled three days in the desert without water. When they finally came to the waters of Marah, they discovered that the water was bitter and undrinkable. Disappointed and afraid, the people blamed Moses and God for their predicament and grumbled against them, saying, "What are we to drink?"

Feeling pressured and threatened by the people, Moses cries out to the Lord, who showed him a piece of wood. When Moses threw the wood into the water, the water became sweet and drinkable and the people's thirst was satisfied.

One of the reasons God shares this account with us is to teach us the cause and cure for bitterness. We've all been to the waters of Marah where we became disappointed and dissatisfied, causing us to grumble about our situation. We, like Israel, have thirsted for satisfaction and, not finding it, our souls were poisoned with bitterness, leaving us helpless and hopeless.

Bitterness is caused by two factors. First comes disappointment. Israel was thirsty and had high hopes when they sighted the waters of Marah, but they were extremely disappointed when they discovered the water was undrinkable. We, too, have high expectations in life that sometimes leads to disappointment. Disappointment by itself, though, whether it be in people, places or circumstances, does not lead to bitterness unless the second factor is brought in, which is blame. Israel blamed Moses, and by extension, God for their situation. Bitterness is almost always directed at someone, blaming them for our disappointment. When you put these two factors together, disappointment and blame, they produce a poison that produces bitterness and eventually kills the soul.

God not only reveals the cause of bitterness, but He also points us to the cure. First, we must remember that it was God Himself who led us to the waters of Marah, the place of our disappointment. It was not an accident or a mistake. God led us there to teach us and bring something good out of our experience. Second, we must believe that God has already provided a cure for our bitterness. Like Moses, we must cry out to God for healing. Third, we ask God to open our eyes to the real purpose of the waters of Marah. Yes, people needed something to drink, but they had a much greater need, learning the secret of trusting God to meet their needs.

The wood that Moses threw into the waters of Marah is a type, or picture, of the cross of Jesus Christ. When we allow the cross of Jesus to impact our lives it has the power to turn the bitter into the sweet, the world's disappointment into God's appointment for our joy.

What does it mean to let the cross impact our lives? It means that we die to our selfish desires and begin living for God's glory. Romans 8:28 tells us, *"And we know that all things work together for the good of those who love Him and are called according to His purpose."*

Do you love Him? Are you living for Him? If so, there is never a reason to be bitter. You can "be joyful always" (1 Th. 5:16), and can "give thanks in all circumstances" (1 Th. 5:18), because you know that God is working something good in your life that is so much better than whatever disappointed you. God's ways are higher than our ways, which means we need to learn to trust Him, even when we can't make sense of what He is doing or where He is leading us.

The cross deals with forgiveness. God forgives our sins because Jesus died for all of them on the cross. When we put our faith in what Jesus did for us on the cross, our sins are cast into the deepest sea, no longer remembered by God. We not only don't get what we deserve, eternal death, but we get what we don't deserve, eternal life. Since our sins against God have been forgiven, it is now possible to forgive those who have sinned against us. Like Joseph, whose brothers sinned against him by selling him into slavery, we can say, *"You intended to harm me, but God intended it for good to accomplish what is now being done, the saving of many lives."* (Gen. 50:20)

When we forgive those who disappoint us, God applies His grace in our lives and it brings a sweetness to our soul.

Week 37

In the Driver's Seat

MY FAMILY AND I WERE traveling a back-country road in my Ford pickup on Joseph Plain in Central Idaho when my 13-year-old son uttered the fateful words, "Dad, can I drive?"

A quick glance at my wife revealed the look of a traitorous conspirator – no help there. Scanning the horizon for a state patrolman proved futile – they're never there when you need them. Even the younger kids, who were in the back of the pickup, deserted me, clamoring for a driving exhibition by the suddenly popular older brother – obviously they were looking forward to a time when their chance to drive would come.

There was no way out.

In the driver's seat, my son pushed the accelerator down and slowly let the clutch out. My heart palpitated faster than the racing engine as I waited for the inevitable lurch. Perhaps he would have done better if I hadn't been sitting closer than a lover, ready to grab the steering wheel in an emergency.

A few lurches later we were traveling down the gravel road. I offered all the advice I knew. "Slow down. Watch out! Speed up. Slow down! Turn. Turn the other way!"

When we finally reached our destination, I wiped the perspiration off my brow and breathed a big sigh of relief and told my son, "Good job."

I couldn't help but notice, though, that the new driver had a look on his face that said, "You didn't trust my driving, Dad." He seemed hurt that I didn't have more faith in him.

Sometimes I wonder if that's the way God feels about us. We say we believe in Him; that we have faith in Him; that we trust him with our lives; but how do we respond when He actually asks for control of our lives?

Many simply say, "No! I'm driving!" Others begrudgingly allow God to get in the driver's seat as they nervously sit alongside, anxiously waiting to grab the steering wheel when they don't like the direction God is taking them. Some tell God, "Okay, you can drive", but they immediately start offering advice, telling God, "Okay, You can go now. Turn here. No, turn there! Slow down. Speed up. Watch out!" Finally, nervous and uncertain where God is taking them, they tell Him, "Okay, let me drive now."

When we question God's direction for our lives, it becomes obvious that we don't really trust Him as we travel this road we call life. We think we can do a better job. We rationalize that we have a better idea how we should live our lives and where we want to go. The truth is, we crave control! We fall for the same lie Satan tempted Eve with, *"you will be like God, knowing good and evil."* (Gen 3:5)

That's foolishness. God is not a teenage novice concerning life. He created us. He knows us. He is more aware of our needs than we are. He knows what is around the next bend in our lives. He knows the way to our intended destination. He is the only one who can guarantee our safe arrival. God deserves to be in the driver's seat of our lives!

All of us have experienced the folly of thinking we can run our lives better than God can. Many of us, if not all, have crashed on the obstacles in our path because we weren't fully trusting God. Solomon offers sound advice when he says, *"Trust in the Lord with all your heart and lean not on your own understanding; in all your ways acknowledge Him, and He will make your paths straight." (Proverbs 3:5-6)*

In a world full of hazards, dangers and accidents, we need to leave the driving to God. If we will only trust Him with our lives, we can sit back, relax, enjoy the trip and be certain we will make our intended destination. Put your faith in God so He can "make your paths straight." (Heb. 12:13)

Week 38

When Good Intentions Are Not Enough

MY NEIGHBOR KENNY IN Keller, Washington, was losing his eyesight and needed a ride to Seattle for a doctor's appointment, so I volunteered to drive him and his wife to Seattle. After performing his tests, the Dr. told Kenny, "You're going blind on account of your drinking. If you quit drinking now, you'll keep the eyesight you have. If you keep drinking, you'll eventually go blind."

Those were sobering words for a long time alcoholic and Kenny was quiet and contemplative as we traveled back home over Snoqualmie Pass. Nearing Ellensburg, I turned on the radio searching for a Christian channel and heard the familiar voice of Chuck Swindoll, who said, "... your wife, your friends, your pastor, even your doctor, have all told you that you need to change ...".

Startled, Kenny looked at me with a look that said, "How did you do that?!"

I shrugged my shoulders, focused on the road and we continued our drive back to the Colville Reservation.

Before we reached Keller, Kenny told me, "I'm going to quit drinking." and I responded, "Praise the Lord!"

The next day some of Kenny's friends stopped by his house and convinced him to have one last party for old time's sake. That one last party lasted six weeks and there wasn't a day during that time that Kenny wasn't drunk. Kenny and his friends drank fifty-two cases of beer after he decided to quit drinking. I prayed for Kenny but wasn't hopeful that anything would change in his life.

Before you come down too hard on Kenny, take some time to reflect on your own 'good intentions'. The truth is, all of us have more 'good intentions' than we do 'good results'. The Apostle Paul sums up our problem in Romans 7:15 where he said, *"I do not understand what I do. For what I want to do I do not do, but what I hate I do."* Paul later attributes our problem to the *"sin living in me."*

Our 'good intentions' are simply not powerful enough to overcome our sinful nature to make the changes that we know are right and necessary. This truth caused Paul to cry out, *"What a wretched man I am! Who will deliver me from this body of death?" (Romans 7:24)* The answer, of course, is "Jesus Christ our Lord."

It took a liver cirrhosis attack before my friend Kenny finally came to the end of himself and cried out to God. Kenny called me on a Saturday morning and asked if I could come to his house and pray for him. When I entered his house, I found Kenny lying on the floor in extreme pain. I shared the Gospel with Kenny and, then, prayed that Kenny would be healed. Kenny confessed his sins to God and asked to be forgiven and saved.

He started feeling better immediately, got up off the floor and sat on the couch where we talked about what it meant to follow Jesus Christ. Like so many before him, Kenny discovered that 'good intentions' are never enough, and that only Jesus Christ has the power to save you and give you victory over sin.

Perhaps you're doing your best to change, but instinctively know that your best can never satisfy the righteous requirements of God. Won't you quit striving and simply put your faith in Jesus Christ. When you give Him control of your life, He not only directs you, but He also gives you the desire and strength to live for Him righteously. Jesus secured the victory on the cross and He promises victory for all who come to Him in life changing faith. It is only in Christ that we can have peace with God and have the desires of our heart satisfied.

Kenny died of diabetes complications a few years after asking Christ to come into his life. It was my prayer then, and now that Kenny is enjoying eternal and abundant life with Jesus Christ now and for eternity. Everything in this life pales in comparison to knowing Jesus Christ and experiencing the glory of Christ forever.

Week 39

Dirt Salad

"THAT'S FUNNY," I THOUGHT. "What's a flowerpot doing on the potluck serving table?" Looking closer, I noticed that half the dirt had been scooped out and someone had spilled fruit salad into the pot. Pointing to the flowerpot, I told the lady in line behind me, "Some kid must not have liked their fruit salad and dumped it into the flowers."

"That's not a flowerpot," she corrected me. "That's Vi's dirt salad. You should try some." Taking a little spoonful, I remarked, "Boy, you never know what you'll find at a church potluck dinner. This is actually pretty good."

Just then, little Amber came through the line. "Ugh! What's that?" she asked with a distasteful look on her face as she pointed at the dirt salad in front of her.

"That's dirt salad," I told her. "you should try some – you'll like it."

Turning really serious and looking somewhat offended, Amber answered, "No, I already ate dirt once and didn't like it." Then, with a determined look on her face, she added, "I'm not eating anymore dirt."

Well, Vi's dirt salad consisted of fruit salad and crushed Oreo cookies, which actually tasted great. Still, little Amber wasn't taking any chances since she ate dirt once before and that was enough for her. The moral is, we should be more like Amber when it comes to spiritual dirt in our lives.

God, who "richly provides us with everything for our enjoyment" (1 Tim. 6:17) has spread out a banqueting table for His people. Out of love, He desires to share His bounty with those He created and all He asks in return is thankfulness and love and obedience.

Unfortunately, Satan brought a real dirt salad to God's banqueting table – we call it sin. He calls out to us, "Sin is sweet, a real treat; try it and you'll feel neat!" We fall for his pitch and, at first, we think, "This is pretty good stuff!" Eventually, though, sin leaves a bitter taste in our mouths and ruins our appetite for the good things God has provided us. It the end, it destroys us from the inside out.

The Apostle Paul asks us, *"What benefit did you reap at that time from the things you are now ashamed of?" (Romans 6:21)* The answer, invariably, is nothing but hurt and ruin.

When we realize this truth, Paul advises us,

> *"Put to death, therefore, whatever belongs to your earthly nature: sexual immorality, impurity, lust, evil desires and greed, which is idolatry. Because of these, the wrath of God is coming. You used to walk in these ways, in the life you once lived. But now you must rid yourselves of all such things as these: anger, rage, malice, slander and filthy language from your lips." (Colossians 3:5-8)*

In effect, Paul is telling us, "You ate dirt in the past and didn't like it, so don't eat it now!"

That's good advice. The next time Satan offers you dirt salad (sin), tell him, "No thanks. I already ate dirt and I don't like it." Then, turn to God and feed on the good things from His banqueting table. God's food satisfies and never leaves us with a bitter taste in our souls. He's inviting us to His banqueting table today, so come and don't delay.

King David challenges us, *"Taste and see that the Lord is good; blessed is the man who takes refuge in Him." (Psalm 34:8).* Take time daily to feed on God's Word and you, too, will be blessed.

Week 40
Who's Watching?

THE FBI AGENT TURNED to the deputy sheriff beside him and asked, "Who's that and what's he doing there?"

"That's my pastor," the deputy answered with surprise written all over his face. "I'm not sure why he is there, but I know he's not involved."

Together they turned and spied on the scene below them. Part of a sting operation, they manned high power video and sound equipment on the hill above town and in a matter of minutes they planned on recording a financial transaction between a suspected arsonist and an undercover agent. That's when I blundered onto the scene.

Earlier, thinking the suspect needed gas for his car, I volunteered to drive him to the nearest service station to fill his five-gallon gas can. Returning to his house, I parked in his driveway, opened my car trunk, and asked him, "Where do you want this gas?"

Pointing to the porch, he watched nervously as I put the can on his step.

Telling him, "Good luck," I got in my car and drove home feeling like the Good Samaritan. Unknown to me, though, everything I did and said was being watched and recorded by the FBI agent on the hill above me.

Later that week the deputy sheriff told me what had transpired on that day. An undercover agent had offered the arsonist money to burn the elementary school down and, as the part-time janitor, the arsonist planned to make it appear that the school's oil furnace had malfunctioned and started the fire.

As it turned out, the deal fell through moments after I left the scene. The arsonist became suspicious, detected a trap and refused to accept the money. The FBI quietly left town, the arsonist barely escaped prison, and I was shocked by what almost happened.

We will all be surprised and shocked when we stand before God and see the detailed recordings of our actions, thoughts, motives and feelings. God is omniscient, which means that He is all-knowing. Nothing escapes His scrutiny and He rewards or punishes us based on the truth. Nothing is hidden from God.

God is not watching us with the intent of punishing us. His greatest desire is our love, and He's watching to see who really does love Him and His Son Jesus. For those who do love Him, God looks forward to the time when He will be able to tell them, "Well done, good and faithful servant. Come and share your Master's happiness." (Mt. 25:21) What a time of rejoicing that will be!

For those who have rejected God's love and lived their lives for themselves, they will be speechless when they stand before Him and He tells them, "Away from Me, you evildoers." (Ps. 119:115) They will be shut out from His Presence for all eternity.

What is God seeing in your life today? If you love Him, He will see obedience and devotion and thanksgiving in your life. If that's missing, you need to question your relationship with God and do everything possible to restore it. God sees your heart and will respond lovingly to any genuine desire to come closer to Him. Seek Him while He may be found.

Week 41

Too Much Freedom

WE WERE GETTING INTO the car to go somewhere when one of my boys exclaimed, "Wait! I think I heard Molly." Molly was our little red and green Love Bird, so we were alarmed. We all jumped out of the car to investigate and, sure enough, there was Molly cavorting high in one of the trees next to our house.

Often, during the day, we let Molly and our Parakeet, Mr. T, loose in our basement so they could enjoy flying around a little. On this day, though, someone left the basement door slightly ajar and Molly made a mad dash towards the wild blue skies and freedom.

What Molly didn't realize, though, was that too much freedom would kill her. Unless we could recaptured her, the little tropical Love Bird would freeze to death that night when the temperature would drop into the high thirties. We were on a mission to save her life!

Molly was enjoying her freedom, though, and wasn't about to give it up easily. The boys chased her from tree to tree until, finally, after climbing seven trees, one of them got close enough to grab her. The Love Bird was returned to her cage where she was snug and warm and safe.

We all enjoy freedom, but too much of it is often dangerous. We know that too much freedom is dangerous for a baby. We would never allow them to play in the medicine cabinet or on the highway because we know they would not survive long. They simply don't have the wisdom or maturity to handle that much freedom.

The same is true for older children. If given too much freedom, they often make bad choices. Many wouldn't eat right, develop good habits, or prepare themselves for adulthood. It would be hard for them to understand why these things are important and they probably would not do them. Most would simply take the easy, enjoyable path and, then, suffer the consequences later.

We might be thinking, "Yes, too much freedom is dangerous for kids, but we're adults, we can handle it." Freedom, though, if not controlled becomes dangerous for us, too. That's why Peter says, *"Live as free men, but do not use your freedom as a cover-up for evil; live as servants of God." (1 Peter 2:16)* When we use our freedom to engage in sin, we become slaves to sin. A short poem summarizes the effects of sin:

Sin will cost you more than you want to pay,
Take you farther than you want to go,
And keep you longer than you want to stay!

Author Anonymous

When we use our freedom to indulge our sinful desires, it becomes dangerous. This is especially true in the area of morals. We're told today, "Throw off the restraints! Don't let anyone tell you what is right or wrong. Decide for yourselves!" Las Vegas encourages sin with the lie, "What happens in Vegas stays in Vegas." Try telling that one to God!

Today we see people who decide it's okay to lie, or steal, or commit sexual immorality. Their motto is, "I did it my way!" Unfortunately, the very freedom they crave is what makes them prisoners. They become enslaved by their sin and lose the ability to experience true love, value and security.

Paul tells us, *"It is for freedom that Christ has set us free. Stand firm, then, and do not let yourselves be burdened again by a yoke of slavery." (Galatians 5:1)* True freedom is the ability and power to do what is right, not whatever we want. When we use our freedom to glorify Jesus Christ in our lives, then we are "free indeed."

Week 42

Out of the Lion's Mouth

FOR THE SECOND TIME in a month our Love Bird, Molly, escaped the safe confines of our home. Like before, we spotted her high in one of the trees next to our home in Cottonwood, Idaho, but, unlike the last time, Molly didn't fly from tree to tree until one of our boys captured her – she simply took off for parts unknown and quickly flew out of sight.

The next day turned cold and wet and we had no illusions of ever seeing Molly again. We were certain it was curtains for our little feathered friend.

A week later I was reading the Cottonwood Chronicle when I noticed an ad that read, FOUND: GREEN AND RED BIRD. CALL (number). We called the number, which happened to be Dr. Sigler, who attended our church, and, as near as we can tell, the following is the amazing story of Molly's rescue.

After leaving our house, Molly flew across town. Shortly after that, Dr. Sigler's wife Amy stepped out her door to walk to the nearest convenience store. Stepping off her porch, Amy noticed her cat had a bird in its mouth and, wanting to save the bird, she chased the cat until it dropped its little feathery prey on the edge of their yard. Hoping to save the bird's life, she tried shooing the bird into the tall grass, when, to her surprise, the bird jumped into her hands. She quickly realized that the Love Bird must be someone's pet, so she put the article in the lost and found section of the paper and it was only a matter of time before we had Molly home safe and sound.

Dr. Sigler's cat, who must have seemed as big as a lion to Molly, miraculously saved her from certain death. I can see many examples of God's providential care for us in our Love Bird's dramatic rescue.

Molly's rescue reminds us that God sees and cares about our troubles. In Luke 12 Jesus taught a crowd about fear and He told them,

> *"Aren't five sparrows sold for two pennies? Yet not one of them is forgotten in God's sight. Indeed, the hairs of your head are all counted. Don't be afraid; you are worth more than many sparrows." (Luke 12:5-6)*

If you are living for God's glory you can be certain that He is working everything out for His glory and for your eternal good. Nothing is impossible with God.

When Daniel's enemies tricked King Darius into passing an edict that banned everyone from praying to anyone other than the king for thirty days, Daniel went into his house, opened his upstairs window and *"three times a day he got down on his knees, prayed, and gave thanks to His God, just as he had done before."* As a result, he was quickly arrested and the King was forced by law to throw Daniel into the lion's den. After a sleepless night, the King ran to the lion's den and cried in anguish to Daniel, *"Daniel, servant of the living God, has your God, whom you continually serve, been able to rescue you from the lions?"* Daniel replied, *"May the king live forever. My God sent his angel and shut the lion's mouths; and they haven't harmed me, for I was found innocent before Him. And also, before you, Your Majesty, I have done no harm."* *(Daniel 6)* Nothing is impossible with God!

Are you experiencing trouble? Maybe it seems like you are in the proverbial "lion's mouth". If you belong to Jesus Christ, you can be sure that He not only cares, but that He is also able to rescue you. David tells

us, *"In the day of my trouble I will call to you, for you will answer me."*
(Psalm 86:7)

Does this mean we will always be delivered from our troubles? No. Sometimes God delivers us out of the troubled waters and sometimes He takes us through the waters, promising *"I will never leave you or forsake you."* Hebrews 11 mentions several heroes of the faith who were delivered and others who suffered and were not delivered. The writer tells us,

> *"All these were approved through their faith, but they did not receive what was promised, since God had provided something better for us, so that they would not be made perfect without us."* *(Hebrews 11:39-40)*

What's promised is eternal life, not a bed of roses.

The cross we bear for Jesus is not our trials or sufferings, but our attitude towards those things – the things that God calls us to die daily to. When we die to self, we experience God's grace in a new dimension, becoming more like Jesus, who was "made perfect through what He suffered for you and I." (Heb. 5:8,9)

Jesus loves us and understands our troubles and, as a result, we can *"approach the throne of grace with confidence, so that we may receive mercy and find grace to help us in our time of need."* *(Hebrews 4:16)*

Week 42
The Wake-Up Call

WHEN WE MOVED FROM Cottonwood, Idaho, to Pony, Montana, we took our little green and red Love Bird Molly with us. Our new church provided us with a modest mobile home to live in and Molly's assigned living arrangement was in my daughter Jennifer's room. Jennifer and Molly had a strong bond, so that worked out well for each of them.

A year later we were contacted by a ministry in Canada that reached out to foreign nationals by giving them excursions in the western U.S. They asked us if we could host one of twenty nationals when they came through our area, and we agreed to put them up for a night.

Our guest was an older Chinese man, who as a world leader in geology, was taking some graduate classes in western Canada. He was a nice, humble man whose English was just passable, so we asked him questions about his life in China. He explained that he and his wife both worked long hours six days a week at a research university. They lived in a small one-bedroom apartment in a high-rise development in their city and they had no children.

Probing deeper, we asked him, "What do you do for fun on your day off?" With a puzzled look on his face, he asked, "What is 'fun'?" It was clear that he had no concept of what 'fun' meant, so we added, "What are your sports or hobbies?" Finally getting our drift, he answered, "We don't do anything for "fun". Our day off is the only time we can clean our apartment, wash our clothes and buy our groceries." Then he added, "We use our day off to get ready for our next week of work."

That night, we took this man to our daughter's bedroom, where he would sleep for the night. We were up early the next day, preparing breakfast, when a scream from our daughter's bedroom startled us.

Alarmed, I asked my wife, "Should we go into the bedroom to see what's wrong?" Before she could respond the bedroom door slammed open and the Chinese man came running out in his pajamas, clearly frightened, stammering something in Chinese. We got him calmed down and he explained in broken English that he was sound asleep when he was attacked by a small green and red bird, which caused him to cry out in alarm and run out of the bedroom. We apologized and explained that our Love Bird must have somehow escaped her cage. He accepted our apology and later left to go back to Canada.

When the kids came home from school, we shared what Molly had done, and Jennifer explained how it happened. "Molly learned how to open her cage door," she explained. "Every morning she opens her door, flies over to my bed, lands on my shoulder and nibbles my ear to wake me up." She laughed and added, "I guess Molly loves to give me a wakeup call!"

Molly must have felt our Chinese guest needed a wakeup call, too!

The truth is: we all need a spiritual wakeup call. This world makes us lethargic spiritually and, if we are not careful, we sleepwalk through our days. Instead of being a beacon of light for Jesus Christ, we walk in the shadows of a dream world, half awake and unresponsive to the leading of the Holy Spirit.

Isaiah 50:4-11 prophesied that Jesus Christ would fulfill His ministry of offering Himself for our sins. In 50:6-7 we read about Christ,

"I gave my back to those who beat me and my cheeks to those who tore out my beard. I did not hide my face from scorn and spitting. The Lord God will help me; therefore, I have not been humiliated; therefore, I have set my face like flint and I know I will not be put to shame."

Facing the pain and humiliation of the Cross, Jesus never wavered, taking our sins and our punishment on Himself. He always did what pleased His Father.

How was Jesus able to fulfill this awful task of saving us? Isaiah 50:4-5 gives us insight into how Jesus was victorious over the desires of the flesh:

"The Lord God has given me the tongue of those who are instructed to know how to sustain the weary with a word. He awakens me each morning; he awakens my ear to listen like those being instructed. The Lord God has opened my ear, and I was not rebellious; I did not turn back."

If Jesus needed to start out His day listening to the voice of His Father, how much more do we need to start our day listening to God's voice. When we wake up each morning, we should whisper a prayer to the Lord, asking Him to speak to our hearts. We should take time to be holy, read a portion of God's Word, meditate on it, ask God to instruct our hearts, and commit ourselves to live for Him that day. If we will do this, I think we will be amazed at the difference it will make in our walk with Jesus.

Week 43
Lucky, My Foot!

AFTER FINISHING AN Easter morning breakfast, we were all ears as Bill shared the details of his latest daring escapade. The day before, with friends watching, Bill flew his ultra-light airplane on its maiden voyage. Hanging by straps from his ultra-light air frame, he was supposed to cut his power when he reached ten feet in elevation and, then, glide gently back to earth as he learned to pilot his aircraft.

Before he realized it, though, he had climbed to eighty feet, where he panicked and cut the engine's power. What was supposed to become a graceful glider suddenly became a demon dive-bomber and plunged into a neighbor's plowed field. His friends, who watched in shock, quickly ran to the wreckage, expecting the worst. Amazingly, though, Bill emerged from the tangled ultra-light virtually unscathed.

Bill summed up his story by stating, "I was just lucky, I guess."

This was too much for me and I couldn't restrain myself. "Lucky, my foot!" I countered. "God was watching over you and that's why you weren't hurt!" No one challenged my assertion and the group quietly broke up, leaving me alone with Bill, who looked at me strangely.

That night I took a call from Bill's wife, who asked, "Are you still starting that new Bible study tomorrow night?" When I replied, "Yes," she told me, "Well, Bill wants to attend." Shocked, I could only mutter, "Okay," not really expecting Bill to show up.

The next night, Bill sat at the table across from me and the host remarked, "I never expected to see you at a Bible study, Bill!" and Bill was quick to respond, "I never expected to be at one, either!"

Five studies later, Bill interrupted the study and asked, "Now let me get this straight. Are you saying that we are either for God or we are against Him?"

When I answered, "That's what the Bible says," Bill replied softly, "That's what I thought you said."

After the study finished, I asked Bill, "Are you for God or against Him?" Bill looked thoughtful and answered, "I think I've been against Him, but I want to be for Him." I explained to Bill the way of salvation and he asked Jesus Christ to come into his heart to forgive him for his sins and to give him a new life for Jesus.

The next day my wife and I went to Bill's house to see his wife about something. Bill was in the yard and when my wife saw him, she remarked, "What happened to Bill?" He had a big smile and his face seemed to glow, so I explained that Bill had been born again the night before.

Bill faithfully served the Lord the next six years until he died of pancreatic cancer. What Bill thought was just luck was God being patient with him and giving him an opportunity to come to Jesus. The Bible tells us, *"He (God) is patient with you, not wanting anyone to perish, but everyone to come to repentance." (2 Peter 3:9)* We're also told in Romans 2:4 that the purpose of God's kindness is to lead us to repentance.

Is it possible that you've had an experience lately where you thought you were just lucky? If so, would you please consider the truth that God is being patient and kind with you, hoping that you will come to Jesus Christ in repentance and faith. His patience doesn't last forever, so ask Christ to be your Lord and Savior while you have the opportunity. You, too, can be on the Lord's side!

Week 45

Jacks

MANY YEARS AGO, WHILE sitting on our couch, my thoughts were interrupted by the excited chatter coming from our dining room. My kids were involved in a heated game of Jacks and their enthusiasm drew me like a magnet.

After watching for a few minutes, I asked, "Can I play, too?"

"Yeah," they replied annoyingly, "but you will have to wait your turn."

Never having played Jacks before, I joined the circle on the floor and concentrated on the game's strategy. "Look's simple," I thought as I watched my oldest son bounce a little rubber ball, pick up four jacks and, then, catch the ball before it hit the ground. When he missed the ball on his next turn, I reasoned to myself, "This will be like taking candy from babies!"

When my turn finally came, I bounced the ball and reached for a single jack, which I missed. "Rats," I mused, "those little buggers aren't easy to grab." The kids laughed at my clumsiness, but I knew that my next turn would be different. It was. I successfully grabbed the jack, but I missed the little ball with my cupped hand.

"Give me another try, "I begged, but my little mockers jeered as they told me, "Wait for your next turn!"

So my evening went. Inept, I realized that Jacks was like any other game – it takes practice to get good at it. I thought, "I'll show you! I'll practice while you're all in school." Unfortunately, the kids hid the jacks, but if I can find them, they'll be surprised the next time I ask, "Can I play too?"

In some ways, life is much like Jacks. We watch a little while and think, "This can't be that hard! With a little practice and luck, I'll do just great." Sooner or later, though, we discover that life isn't as easy as it seems and we find ourselves struggling.

The same is true in our walk with Christ. He comes into our lives as Lord and Savior and asks us to follow Him. "No problem," we think. "How hard can it be to be loving, kind, patient, thoughtful and helpful?" When we finally get our turn to practice Christ-likeness, we painfully fall on our face when our old self rears its ugly head up with its self-centered infatuation. Humiliated, but not deterred, we reason, "It will be different next time!", but it's not. After many failures many Christians simply give up because the failures are too painful.

What we've failed to realize, though, is that the Christian life is just like most other endeavors – it takes practice to succeed. It isn't easy to love my neighbor as myself; it's difficult to be kind to others when we feel annoyed; it's next to impossible to be patient when we are in a hurry. After a while we begin to discover that none of Christ's traits are going to come naturally into our lives.

That's why Paul advises us, *"Whatever you have learned or received or heard from me, or seen in me – put it into practice. And the God of peace will be with you."* (Phil. 4:9) Godliness takes practice! When we fail, we shouldn't give up in discouragement, but remember, *"I can do everything through Him who gives me strength."* (Phil. 4:13)"

Instead of becoming discouraged when we fall, we should get up and resolve, "I'll do better next time." If we'll do that, with God's help, we'll start to notice a change taking place in our lives. It may be gradual at first, but before we know it, the results of our practice will start to become more evident. Others will experience the blessings of the change in our lives and Christ will receive the glory.

If we make the commitment to keep going, no matter how hard it is, we'll soon discover that the old adage "Practice makes perfect" is really true.

Week 46

The Empty Gun

HUNTING SEASON HAD arrived with its high hopes and great expectations for my son John and me. With a little skill and luck (maybe more of the latter), the "great White Hunters" would fill the freezer with venison and elk steaks.

A friend from our church invited us to hunt on his ranch bordering the Salmon River in north central Idaho, which was prime deer hunting territory. When I told the friend that my son John wanted to hunt, also, but I only had one rifle, he told me, "You can borrow mine."

We arrived at the ranch before sunrise and my friend told us the best places to find deer. He handed me his rifle and informed me that the magazine was full of bullets. After leaving his house, I chambered a cartridge and we began our hunt as the sun came up over the mountains to the east.

We flushed out three deer right away and I managed a shot at one of them, but the rising sun blurred my scope and I missed (any excuse is as good as another!). "No problem," I thought as I ejected the spent casing, "there's plenty more deer here."

Well, we hunted and hunted and saw deer and more deer, but we were never able to get close enough for a shot. Finally, weary and cold, we tromped back to my friend's ranch house as darkness descended around us. After reporting our failure to bag a deer, I decided to empty his gun and give it back to him. Pulling the bolt back, I was surprised when no cartridge came out of the chamber. Peering into the empty chamber, I exclaimed, "Well, can you beat that. I've been hunting with an empty gun all day!"

Now you and I both know that hunting with an empty gun is an exercise in futility. All the sneaking around, stalking the prey, and setting up good shots are meaningless without bullets in your gun. Even the best hunter in the world can't shoot a deer with an empty gun - ammunition is essential!

Hunting with an empty rifle seems silly, but not near as silly as someone trying to live the Christian life empty of the Spirit of God in them. The Apostle Paul declares, "*And if anyone does not have the Spirit of Christ, he does not belong to Christ.*" (Romans 8:9b)

How does the Spirit of Christ enter a person? It doesn't happen through some kind of magic or religious rite. A person can belong to a church, be baptized and receive communion and still not have the Holy Spirit in their life. God isn't manipulated or fooled by our false piety, incomplete repentance and religious works.

The Holy Spirit enters our lives when we put our full and complete trust in Jesus and make a commitment to follow Him, no matter what the cost. Having given up on yourself and your best efforts to satisfy God's demand for complete holiness, you put your trust in Jesus Christ and what He did for you on the Cross, dying in your place, taking your sins upon Himself, and satisfying the wrath of God that all of us fully deserved. Believing that He paid the penalty for your sins, you desire to live for Him out of thanksgiving for what He did for you.

When we repent and cry out to God for forgiveness of our sins, the Holy Spirit enters our lives as a pledge and guarantee that God will accomplish His work in your life, making you more and more like Jesus. The Bible calls this experience the "new birth." Jesus told the religious leader Nicodemus, "*I tell you truth, unless a man is born again, he cannot see the kingdom of God.*" and "*I tell you the truth, unless someone is born of water and the Spirit, he cannot enter the Kingdom of God.*" (John 3:3 & 5)

2 Corinthians 13:5 challenges all of us when it says, "*Examine yourselves to see whether you are in the faith; test yourselves. Do you not realize that Christ Jesus is in you - unless, of course you fail the test.*" If you are in Christ, then you will be producing the Fruit of the Spirit (love, joy, peace patience, kindness, goodness faithfulness, gentleness and self-control - Gal. 5:22) and God will be glorified in your life

If you don't see this fruit growing in your life, ask God to forgive your sin of rebellion and self-rule and invite Jesus Christ to come into your life to be your Lord and Savior. He promises that He will save all who call upon Him and He will be faithful to fulfill His plan for your life. He is worthy!

Week 47

Are You Listening?

IT SEEMED THAT FIVE P.M. would never arrive, but when it did that Friday night, I left work, hopped in my van, drove out of Aberdeen and headed for Spokane. My family, including my new two-week old daughter Jennifer, had been visiting at Grandma's house, and I really missed them after the two weeks absence.

Unknowingly to me, this trip would completely change my life.

Driving on I-90 East through the night, I reflected on the good things God was doing in my life. My wife and children loved me; my job at Ocean Spray Cranberries fulfilled me; we had recently gotten out of debt; my church, Copalis Community Church, accepted me and stretched my faith; and I felt positive about my future. My reflections gradually turned to praise as I began to thank God for His love for me, which He had expressed to me by allowing His Son Jesus to die for my sins.

Suddenly a thought broke through my consciousness and I understood immediately that God had spoken to me.

"Now," God said clearly.

Instinctively understanding that "now" meant that I was to devote my life to fully serving God, I responded, "Not now, Lord! Things are going too well in my life." Then I added, "Why not later?"

"Now," God repeated, much quieter, and I knew that my answer would determine the course of the rest of my life. I answered with a meek, "Yes, Lord," and made the decision to follow Jesus Christ no matter what the consequences would be. It was the wisest decision I ever made.

That next morning, I shared my experience with my wife, telling her that I believed God wanted me to quit my job, finish Bible School and go into the ministry. I expected her to be concerned and worried about the financial security of our growing family, but she surprised me when she answered, "I've been praying for that for a long time!"

That decision was made forty years ago this month (October), and I am so glad that God spoke to me that night. If He hadn't, I would have quit the ministry dozens of times because of frustrations and failures. As it stands, though, there has been no doubt about what God wants me to do because He told me. That's real security, knowing that I am in the center of God's will for my life.

God still speaks today. Hebrews 1:2 tells us, *"In these last days, He has spoken to us by His Son."* He mainly speaks to us through His Word about Jesus and we need to read and hear it with the desire to hear His voice. There may be times or occasions, though, when God speaks to us directly for our encouragement, correction or direction and we need to be in a loving relationship with Jesus, so we can hear His voice clearly.

In Revelation 3:20 Jesus invites us to listen to Him. He says, *"Here I am! I stand at the door and knock. If anyone hears my voiced and opens the door, I will come in and eat with him and he with me."*

Christ is looking for that intimate fellowship where we sit at His feet and enjoy sweet communion together. He loves us and wants to spend quality time with us so we can know and love Him better.

Most of us have experienced the frustration of talking to someone who won't listen. Can you imagine how Christ must feel when He longs to share His love, but people won't listen to Him? How foolish!

Hebrews warns us, *"Today if you hear His voice, do not harden your hearts."* The wise person listens to God and obeys His Word. Are you listening today?

Week 48

The Trestle

"IMPRESSIVE," I REMARKED, viewing the railroad trestle for the first time. Old, decaying, and abandoned, it stood as a mute testimony to the logging trains that carried logs from the flanks of Mount Saint Helens to the mills in nearby Longview. Discarded and dangerous, we had been hired to dismantle the trestle and salvage the one-hundred-foot cedar logs.

The eight columns of five logs stood like a troop of tall, dignified soldiers in the middle of the mountain ravine. "Cut each one of them off at the base," our boss instructed us, "and we'll pull them over with the winch truck."

We sawed through the forty-inch-thick butts of each pole, hooked up the winch cable and pulled, expecting the whole structure to come tumbling down. To our surprise, the trestle never even budged – the support planks that connected each column were just too strong.

Frustrated by the delay in his plans, the boss gave me the job of cutting the support planks that joined the columns together while the rest of the crew moved to another trestle farther up the mountain.

Starting at the base of the second column I cut the five 3"X12" planks that connected it to the first column. I repeated this procedure at the twenty, forty, sixty, eighty and one-hundred-foot levels until the first column was completely separated from the rest of the trestle. Duplicating the process, I eventually reach the eighth and final column.

Working up the final column, I began sawing the last cross support on the one-hundred-foot level when my brain flashed an alert – "When you cut this plank," it warned me, "there's nothing holding the column up and keeping it from falling over!"

Instantly trembling, I quit sawing. Worried that the slightest movement might cause the column to fall, sweat broke out on my brow as I pondered my situation. The slight breeze that I had enjoyed seconds earlier now seemed like a hurricane intent on destroying me. Almost paralyzed with a sudden fear of heights, I cautiously inched down the column. Finally reaching the ground, I breathed a sigh of relief and offered a silent prayer of thanksgiving. Never had earth felt so good to me as it did at that moment.

All of us have been delivered from dangerous situations at one time or another in our lives. Instead of passing this off as luck or skill, we should give God the credit and praise Him. Then, instead of taking our rescue for granted, we should devote our lives to the One who loved us and saved us. Like Paul, who was delivered from many dangers, we should say, *"The Lord will rescue me from every evil attack and will bring me safely to his heavenly kingdom. To Him be glory for ever and ever. Amen." (2 Tim. 4:18)*

Week 49

What's Your Destination?

I HUNG UP THE PHONE and hollered to my family, "Okay, I've got the directions. Let's go!" We were going to visit trapper Brown and his wife, who lived thirty miles north of the Yellowstone River in some of the most barren and desolate country of Eastern Montana.

We jumped in the station wagon, crossed the Yellowstone River, traveled north out of Forsyth until we turned onto the Little Porcupine Creek Road, which was a dirt track that led off into the barren hills that seemed to go on forever. We felt confident about our destination until we came to a fork in the road and I couldn't remember if we were supposed to turn right or left. The road to the right was narrow and little used while the road to the left was broad and well-traveled. After some consideration, I chose the well-traveled road and we continued our trip.

We followed the road for ten miles when it abruptly ended at a pasture where a rancher was feeding his cattle. Not seeing any houses nearby, I asked the rancher for directions to the Brown's home. He pointed back the way we had come and told us, "Go back this road ten miles and turn onto the narrow road. You can't miss them."

Somewhat embarrassed, we traveled back to the Y in the road, turned onto the narrow road that led to the Brown's, eventually arrived and had a great visit.

Our trip to the Brown's that day is symbolic of our trip through life. We are all traveling life's highways and byways and there are only two directions that we can go – our way or God's way. Jesus tells us,

> *"Enter through the narrow gate. For wide is the gate and broad is the road that leads to destruction, and many enter through it. But small is the gate and narrow the road that leads to life, and only a few find it."* (Mt. 7:13-14)

Concerning the broad way, Proverb's 16:25 tells us, *"There is a way that seems right to a man, but in the end, it leads to destruction."* The "broad way", or our way, seems "right", but it never leads us to eternal life. Sooner or later our way fizzles out and leaves us puzzled by a life that led nowhere. People travel the broad way because it seems sensible and easy, with lots of company. People on the broad way may be moral, or immoral; friendly or unfriendly; religious or irreligious; but they all have one thing in common – they are all going the wrong way and it leads to hell.

On the other hand, there are those who are traveling the narrow road. Jesus tells us that few find it and that it is hard, but it leads to eternal life. There is only one way to enter this road, which is Jesus Christ, and you have to take up your cross daily in order to follow Him. Those on the broad road may ridicule and despise you, but it doesn't matter because the narrow road leads to eternal life in Christ Jesus.

These truths were brought home to me one day when Mrs. Helen Baugh, the founder and director of Christian Women's Clubs, visited us in Rosebud, Montana. She brought everything into perspective when she said, "Everyone in this town has a destination – either heaven or hell."

What is your destination? Do you sense an emptiness in your life? Are you worried that maybe the road you are following is going the wrong way? If so, it's not too late to turn to Jesus and follow Him on the road that leads to life. The road will be narrow and you may not have a lot of company, but you have Jesus' promise that He will "*never leave you or forsake you*" (Heb. 13:5) and He will "*carry to completion the work He began in you.*" (Phil. 1:6)

If you have entered this road, are you making every effort to stay on the straight and narrow? If so, your progress will be a tremendous testimony to others who need to join you as you follow Jesus and you will experience real joy in your life.

Week 50

The Difference

MANY PEOPLE POINT TO the different religions of the world and proclaim that they are all useful and valuable because they all point to a Higher Power. They reason in their minds that there maybe one God, but there are many roads, or paths, to reach Him. Islam, Buddhism, Hinduism, Confucianism, etc., all claim that they are useful in providing a pathway through life that will lead to fulfilment, both in the here and now and the hereafter. As such, they claim equality with Christianity.

Are their claims valid? Are they just different roads to the same place? Do they all bring us to God? Is there any difference? Possibly the best way to answer these questions is to look at each leader's tomb.

Mohammed's tomb - - - - - - - - - OCCUPIED
Buddha's tomb - - - - - - - - - - - OCCUPIED
Confucius's tomb - - - - - - - - - - OCCUPIED
Jesus Christ's tomb - - - - - - - - EMPTY!

The difference, as the angel put it when the women came to the tomb to anoint Jesus body for burial, is, *"He is not here; He has risen!"* (Mt. 28:6) All other religions, including humanism and animism, put their hope in what man can do for himself; they attempt to elevate man in some way. Only Christianity says, "There is nothing I can do to satisfy the righteous demands of a Holy God – I don't have the resources to do it. Therefore, I must rely on God to satisfy His demands of holiness for me."

That is why it was necessary for Christ Himself to come to this earth to pay the penalty that a Holy God demanded for sin. Christ paid for our sins when He died on the cross. To prove that the penalty had been paid in full, it was necessary for Christ to rise from the dead. His resurrection proved beyond a shadow of a doubt that He was victor over sin and death. Because Jesus lives, we also can live in Him.

Christians are often accused of being bigoted and dogmatic over this issue. People protest, "Christians don't seem willing to compromise." If Christ has been raised from the dead, though, how can this truth be compromised. It is our only hope of living for eternity. Christ Himself claimed, "I am the way and the truth and the life. No one comes to the Father except through Me." When the disciples were struggling with Jesus teaching about eating His body and drinking His blood (He was referring to the spiritual), many turned away from following Him. He turned to the twelve and said, *"You don't want to go away too, do you?"* Simon Peter answered, *"Lord, to whom will we go? You have the words of eternal life. We have come to believe and know that you are the Holy One of God."* (Jn. 6:67, 68)

Jesus is the only One in all of history who has risen from the dead and He alone is uniquely qualified to give eternal life to all who come to Him in faith. Our Savior is alive and is sitting at the righthand of God interceding for us. Because He lives, we also will live. He's alive!

As you celebrate Easter you can give Christ no better gift than yourself. Christ died for our sin so that we might be dead to sin and alive to God. The hope of Easter is not the new life of spring, but New Life in Christ. That's the difference that makes Easter worth celebrating.

Week 51

A Perilous Trek

MY FIRST WIFE JAN BATTLED cancer for sixteen years, eventually losing her life to it in 2005. My second wife Sondra experienced a worse cancer, but she defeated it, and has been cancer free for twenty-six years. Cancer is scary.

Facing cancer is similar to visiting a **Foreign Country**. Cancer forces you to leave the safe and secure **Land of Health**, with an emotional farewell, and to embark on a scary and, often, painful journey through the **Land of Treatment**.

Often, you land on the **Shores of Treatment** at the **Port of Surgery**. Although they try to be hospitable, **Surgeons**, as the local residents are called, usually poke and prod you until your body is black and blue and sore in ways you never imagined before visiting there. You hear many greetings, such as, "This will only sting a little bit", or "This shouldn't cause too much discomfort", but you soon learn to discount their optimism as a vain attempt to encourage you during your stay. Upon leaving the **Port of Surgery**, many visitors comment, "Unpleasant, but bearable."

Your itinerary continues with a side trip to the **Swampy Lowland of Chemotherapy**. A poisonous district, many visitors feel sick there. Often, visitors can be identified by their bald heads, sickly pallor, and drowsy behavior. Not exactly a resort city, many visitors somehow leave the **Land of Chemotherapy** healthier than when they arrived. Evidently, they experience some kind of purging while they visit there.

Unfortunately, many visitors find themselves in the **Valley of Despair**, which seemingly goes on forever. Others, who have passed this way, assure them that there is an exit at the **Tunnel of Light** at the end of the **Valley**, but it is still slow going and very monotonous for those waiting to see the **Light of Day** at the other end of the **Tunnel**.

There are many other trips taken in this **Land of Treatment**, but, hopefully, the next stop is the **Plateau of Recovery**. Visitors here feel healthy and exuberant, enjoying activities and scenery that excite their souls. Most travelers linger here as long as possible before they continue their journey because it is a pleasant place.

Whether they travel over the **Plateau of Recovery** or not, all travelers eventually reach the **Valley of the Shadow of Death**. Dark and dangerous looking, this **Valley** appears to be the end of the of the journey, but it isn't. Although they aren't easily visible, there are **Two Doors** that lead the traveler on to their **Eternal Destination**.

One door is wide, but it leads to **Eternal Destruction**. This door is labeled "**Self-Centered**". The other door is narrow, but it leads to **Eternal Life**. This door is labeled "**Christ Centered**."

If you enter the **Wide Door of Eternal Destruction,** you land in the **Lake of Fire,** which fills the **Pit of Hell**, where there is darkness, torment, and loneliness. God doesn't want anyone to go there, but most ignore Him and do what seems right to them, which eventually separates them from the **Love of God**.

The few who enter the **Narrow Door,** which is labeled **Christ Centered**, discover that they have come to the **Celestial City**, where they meet **King Jesus**, who tells them,

"Well done, good and faithful servant! You have been faithful with a few things; I will put you in charge of many things. Come and share your master's happiness! (Mt. 25:23)

You may not be facing cancer or some other life-threatening illness, but all of us are traveling through the **Country of Life**. If you have been more concerned about the journey than the destination, please stop a moment and reconsider your priorities. If you are traveling the **Easy Road to Hell**, it's not too late to change your destination. All you have to do is look to Jesus Christ, repent of your rebellion against Him, and ask Him to lead you on the **Road to Heaven**. He is faithful to guide you the whole trip, ensuring that you will spend eternity with Him. **Jesus is a faithful guide who will lead you safely home.**

May God guide and direct you in this journey we call life!

Week 52
The Big "C"

CANCER. EVEN THE WORD scares you, as my first wife Jan and I found out thirty years ago (January 1990).

Jan hung up the phone after talking with her mother Hazel and then turned to me with a worried look. "Mom's having a biopsy for cancer next week," she informed me. "Can I go to Spokane to be with her and drive her to the doctor and back?"

"Sure," I responded sympathetically. "Your mom needs you at a time like this."

The doctors performed the biopsy on Tuesday, and Hazel found out her test results on Thursday. After taking her mom home from the doctor, Jan drove back home to Cottonwood, Idaho, and arrived just before our evening Bible study was ready to begin in our home.

When she walked into the house I anxiously asked, "How did your mom's biopsy go?"

"Not good," she replied. "She's having surgery next Tuesday." Looking tired and worn out, she paused a moment and added, "I need to talk to you alone."

Finding a place to be by ourselves, she shared, "I asked the doctor to look at the lump on my breast today and he did a quick needle biopsy." Then with tears in her eyes, she whispered quietly, "I have cancer, too."

Stunned, I hugged her and wondered, "How is this possible? She saw a doctor four years ago who told her he didn't think the lump she had was cancerous. She had a mammogram that same year and another one recently, and neither were positive for cancer."

Then a new thought hit me. "My mother died of cancer twenty years ago this same month! Is Jan going to die?" Fear began mounting up within me as I realized that cancer – the big "C" – had trespassed in our home.

We didn't have time to comfort each other, because people started filtering in for our scheduled Bible study. We sang a few songs to the Lord. Then I announced, "We're going to change our format tonight because we have some bad news." Attentive, they listened as I shared, "Jan and her mom both have cancer and will have surgery in Spokane next Tuesday."

It's hard to describe what followed. We cried, we prayed, we shared Scripture promises, we laughed, and we hugged. God met us in our little group and we felt His presence, love and security." Yes, the big "C" had hit us, but we discovered that God had even bigger "C's" to help us. We experienced the "C's" of comfort and compassion and they were enough to help us, despite our concerns, questions and fears about our future.

We experienced the truth of 2 Cor. 1:3-4, where Paul says, *"Praise be to the God and Father of our Lord Jesus Christ, the Father of compassion and the God of all comfort, who comforts us in all our troubles."*

Jan and her mom had surgery on the same day by the same doctor in the same hospital and shared the same room for their recovery. Jan's mom remarked, "This is the first time you and I have been in the same hospital room since the day you were born."

Jan and her mom followed different paths after their surgeries. Hazel recovered completely and lived another 30 years. Jan's cancer came back 6 years later. Although the cancer eventually claimed her life, she won the victory and stayed faithful to God until the day she died. God's promise, *"I will never leave nor forsake you"* (Heb. 13:5) gave her great comfort and courage and she won the victory.

We don't know if or when we may face adversity in our lives, but if we know Jesus Christ we believe and know we will obtain the promises God has given us through Jesus Christ. Like the Apostle Paul, who was facing death in the arena, we can say, *"I know whom I have believed, and am convinced that He is able to guard what I have entrusted to Him for that day."* (2 Timothy 1:12)

Week 53

Fighting the Good Fight

THINGS CHANGE. I KNOW because I experienced this reality early in 1997.

My first wife, Jan, and I walked on the beach that February and the bright sun made the waves shimmer like diamonds. We lived for days like that on the coast of the Olympic Peninsula here in Washington, but I couldn't appreciate them on that day. We hiked north towards the mouth of the Copalis River with the pounding surf on our left and bleached driftwood on our right, with a wonderful past behind us and an uncertain future in front of us.

Much was the same in our lives, but much was also different. Instead of our normal two miles, Jan asked to stop and sit down after 300 yards because her chest hurt. We found a log to sit on where we would pray for our family, church and community. We had been doing this in different places since I entered the ministry seventeen years earlier and it had become an important part of our life and ministry.

I tried to pray but I could only cry. The events of the last month weighed heavy on my heart and the shortened walk brought reality too close to the surface. Finally, staring at the ocean waves and choking back tears, I asked Jan, "If you only had six months to live and could only do one thing, what would you do?"

Since this wasn't idle talk, Jan thought deeply as I contemplated the past. God had blessed our twenty-four years together with love and friendship, four wonderful children, fulfilling relationships and ministries, and a growing sense of His Presence in our lives. I had recently written in my diary, "Sometimes it seems that our lives and personalities have become so intermeshed that 'Jim and Jan' really are one person, not two."

Now, after chest pains in December and extensive tests in January, we learned that Jan's 1990 breast cancer had metastasized to her right lung and pleura. The doctor had informed us that she had untreatable, incurable, terminal cancer. The news hung like a heavy millstone around our necks, threatening to drag us down into despair.

Jan answered my question about what she wanted to do with longing in her eyes when she told me, "If I could do anything I wanted, I would go back to Russia. I still feel like God has something for me to do there."

This was so like Jan, I thought. Instead of worrying about her cancer, she was thinking about what she could do for the Lord. She shared later that God had prepared her for this time through a women's Bible study on Corinthians. She knew that He had promised that "our light and momentary troubles are achieving for us an eternal glory that far outweighs them all."

She told a friend, "I haven't had to fight this battle alone. So often, a call or a visit or a card or a helping hand or a prayer comes at just the right time. Church walls or denominational lines do not hinder this awesome working of the body of Christ." Then she added, "This amazes and humbles me."

So, Jan waited on the Lord. Would she go to Russia? She believed that God could provide a way for her to go. Meanwhile, she was excited every day to see what God would do in her life. Obviously, we prayed for a miracle healing, but, as she commented to a friend one day, "If God were to heal me and not do a work in me and in the church, I'm not sure it would be worth it."

Sooner or later, all of us face an uncertain future, where sunny days can be obscured by stormy clouds in a matter of moments. It's times like these that reveal where we have placed our hope. If our hope is based on our circumstances, we are bound to crumble under the crushing weight of bad news. If our hope is based on Jesus Christ and his love for us, we will shine like the stars in the sky on a dark night, bringing glory to our Heavenly Father.

Jesus understood this. When He faced the horror of the crucifixion he prayed, "I have brought you glory on earth by completing the work you gave me to do. And now, Father, glorify me in your presence with the glory I had with you before the world began." (Jn. 17:4, 5)

Whether in life or death, Jan wanted God to be glorified in her life. He certainly was. Is that the desire of your heart?

Week 54
You Will Not Die, But Live!

I WAS AMAZED AT THE intensity of the lady's prayer! We were standing in a small living room in a dingy, concrete apartment building in Perm, Russia, which is a city of about 1.4 million people, one thousand miles northeast of Moscow. The trip to Perm was a miracle for my wife, Jan, who had been diagnosed with terminal cancer in February of that year, 1997. Her one desire had been to go back to Russia and minister in the land she loved and, now, God had answered her prayer.

Sitting there in the small Russian living room, I marveled at these strangers' sincere desire for my Jan's healing, I couldn't help but give thanks to God. Just the night before we had been in another home group meeting as Russian Christians shared a meal with us and then fervently prayed for Jan.

The group of eighteen prayed for a half hour when our interpreter, twenty-one-year old Irene, excitedly told us that God had given her a verse for Jan. Later, she discovered that God had given another lady the same verse and she was doubly excited!

I waited anxiously to discover what the verse, *Psalm 118:17*, had to say to Jan. You can imagine our joy in reading, "*You will not die, but live, and will proclaim what the Lord has done.*" (Ps. 118:17) We took this as a promise from the Lord and praised Him for His kindness to us.

Now, the following evening, I watched in amazement as this lady cried out to God for Jan for ten minutes, then went down on her knees in front of Jan for another ten minutes, imploring God in Russian for His favor. Then she stood, lifting Jan's hands into the air for another ten minutes with the most impassioned prayer I had ever heard. When she finally finished praying, she embraced Jan in what seemed a victory hug and I thought, "Wow! God has done something special here."

Jan told the group about the verse she received the evening before and promised, "When I get home I'm going to my doctor and will report his findings to you."

Healed or not, our trip was wonderful! We almost didn't get into Russia, because the Russian consulate in Seattle made a mistake on our Visa dates. The authorities pulled us out of line at customs in Moscow and told us we would have to return home. Sitting there all by ourselves underneath a sign that read, "Don't tell me you didn't bring your Visa card (credit) with you", we prayed, sang and did spiritual warfare, knowing that "He who was in us is greater than he who is in the world." (1 Jn. 4:4) Finally, after two hours of waiting and a hundred and fifty-dollar fine, they gave us permission to continue our trip.

And what a trip it was! We rode the train 20 hours to Perm, enjoying the beautiful countryside and quaint villages. We taught four days together in a Bible school; visited five orphanages, where we handed out gifts to the beautiful Russian children and Jan shared Jesus' story about the Lost Sheep; preached the Gospel at two different churches; and shared at two home group meetings. We participated in Russian life with our hosts Aleg, Ilene and ten-year-old Julia; explored Perm, learning how to ride the buses and trams that crisscrossed the city; and marveled at God's goodness to us in a land so far away from home.

More than anything, though, we would remember the vibrant, sacrificial love for Jesus Christ that the Russian Christians displayed. The pastors and church leaders, who were all in their twenties, had established a strong church of 1600, started a Bible school that all new converts had to attend, and planted forty-eight churches in the surrounding area over the previous six years, all with young pastors that they had led to Jesus and trained. We marveled at God's amazing power to accomplish such a great work in such a short time. They seemed on fire as they served God with all their heart.

When we arrived home, Jan scheduled an appointment with her oncologist. When he saw her, he exclaimed, "Wow! I thought you had died." After examining Jan, the oncologist told her, "If I didn't know where to look for the cancer, I would say that you didn't have any." Then, he added, "Whatever you are doing, keep doing it!"

Jan would live another six years with relatively good health before the cancer finally exerted itself and eventually took her life in December of 2004. During that time, she continued to serve God and proclaim His goodness in the land of the living. Her life was a tremendous encouragement to many and a testimony to God's love for all of us. She eventually died after sixteen years of fighting her disease, but even in dying she glorified Jesus who died for Her and paid for her sins. She won the victory!

Week 55
A Day No Rain Would Fall

AFTER A WEEK OF RAIN and clouds, December 8th, 2004, arrived bright and sunny in Copalis Beach, Washington. Jan, who loved the sun and simply tolerated the gloomy, overcast weather on the Washington coast, had slipped into a coma earlier that morning, unfazed by clouds or her inability to breathe. She had fought her cancer with surgery, chemotherapy, radiation, homeopathy, diet, exercise and prayer, lots of prayer, for the last eighteen years and the battle would end peacefully and victoriously that day.

The cancer had raised its ugly head many times, seemingly ready to destroy Jan, but God, who is rich in mercy, always provided a way of escape. Her endurance in the face of pain, tiredness and discouragement was a testimony to God's strength, which worked so powerfully in her. When faced with overwhelming odds, she continually responded, "But God ..."

What Satan planned for evil, God worked for good. Fear often encircled her like shadows around a campfire at night, but it only drove her closer to the Light, where she always found safety and security. She woke up early to pray, crying out to God in her church or walking the streets of Copalis Beach, interceding for its residents. Women sensed her power in prayer, knowing her familiarity in the throne room of God, and beat a path to her door, asking for intercession, wisdom and advice.

Jan loved the Word, the Bread of Life, and spent hours each day digging for Pearls of Wisdom in its pages, with colored pens and markers bearing witness to her diligence and determination. God had told her 25 years earlier that *"You need to persevere so that when you have done the will of God, you will receive what He has promised."* (Hebrews 10:36)

She never wavered. Nine days before meeting her God, she led a woman's Bible study on the Holy Spirit; two days before going home, she hosted a women's Bible study in her home, listening from her hospital bed; the day before she saw Jesus, she fought through mental confusion and feasted on God's promises.

In January of 1997 the doctors confirmed that Jan's breast cancer had metastasized to her right lung. If she took treatment, she was told, she might have two years to live. She refused treatment, unwilling to surrender to the cancer and, like Hezekiah's response to the Assyrian king, threw herself on the mercy of the Living God, who alone can give and take life.

God gave her nine wonderful years, allowing her to go on mission trips to Russia (twice), Honduras (four times), Mexico, and Los Angeles (four times); to see two children marry and three grandsons born, one that she helped deliver in her own home; to teach women's Bible studies and children's Sunday school classes; and to develop exciting relationships with so many people.

She and her husband, Jim, experienced a wonderful intimacy during that time, growing more and more in love, enjoying each other's presence and company. They took hiking trips in the Olympic Mountains, played board games, entertained friends and family, walked on the beach, picked wild blackberries and mushrooms, sang hymns together on quiet evenings at home, and simply served each other in times of need.

Eventually, the cancer began to decimate Jan's body, but her face became more and more unveiled, reflecting the Lord's glory, which amazed people who saw her. Like the great apostle Paul, she could claim,

> *"For I am already being poured out as a drink offering, and the time has come for my departure. I have fought the good fight, I have finished the race, I have kept the faith. Now there is in store for me the crown of righteousness, which the Lord, the righteous judge, will award to me on that day – and not only to me, but also to all who longed for his appearing."* (2 Timothy 4:6-8)

Several of us were singing hymns to Jan when she slipped into eternity. No, Jan didn't see the sun that day, but she did see the Son, Jesus Christ, gazing on his beauty, embraced by his love, giving thanks for his salvation and singing his praises for eternity. As friends of the Bridegroom, we can rejoice that he found a bride so beautiful and we can prepare for that day when we will see the King as well.

Week 56

No Crying

THE WEEK AFTER MY FIRST wife Jan's funeral, in December 2005, my oldest son Justin and I drove to Wilmington, California, where my third son Jeremy and his wife Stacy served with *FriendShips Ministries* in the LA Harbor area. I hoped the daily busy work in the *FriendShips* warehouse would help heal the grief of losing my wife of thirty-two years.

After two weeks of busy days and mostly sleepless nights, Jeremy asked if I was willing to help drive one of two cars to the *FriendShips* headquarters in Lake Charles, Louisiana. A road trip seemed like a good diversion, so I agreed. We left Louisiana and traveled 1600 miles in two days to Lake Charles, where I bunked by myself in a small room on the *Spirit of Grace*, an old 350-foot freighter that the ministry used to deliver supplies to third world countries.

Again, days were busy with different chores and nights were filled with sorrow. Almost a week into my stay there, still grieving, I felt a need to go outside onto the deck and talk to the Lord.

Standing on the port side of the third deck, I noticed a picnic table, reminding me that Jan and I had been at that table five years earlier when we had visited Jeremy in Roatan, Honduras. All of a sudden, in my mind's eye, I saw a vision of the whole crew and Jan sitting at this table as I led them in a morning devotional, which I did every morning when we were there.

My vision seemed real and I was excited about seeing Jan, but just as quickly as the vision came, it vanished. I started to cry. That's when I reminded myself of a promise I made to God before Jan died, "No, I said I wasn't going to cry, but was going to worship the Lord no matter what happened."

I lifted my hands to the clear, beautiful starry Louisiana night and began praising the Lord, thanking Him for the thirty-two years He had given Jan and I, praising Him for His goodness to me despite my loss, and committing myself to serving Him no matter what I faced in the future. Then, with my eyes focused on the heavens, God spoke to me with a loving voice, telling me, "You loved your wife Jan, and you did everything you could for her, but she isn't coming back."

Suddenly, a peace flooded through my soul. Even today it is hard to express what I experienced, but I felt an immediate release from the pain of the past and felt a tremendous excitement about the future. I quickly went back to my room and scheduled a flight from Houston to Louisiana the next day so I could drive home to Copalis Beach. Then I called one of my church elders and asked him to let the church know I would be home for the worship service that Sunday.

I experienced firsthand that night what Isaiah 26:3-4 promised: *"You will keep in perfect peace him whose mind is steadfast, because he trusts in you. Trust in the Lord forever, for the Lord, the Lord is the Rock eternal."*

Sooner or later our lives are shaken by events that we have no control over and it is during these times that we discover who or what we are trusting in. Isaiah described the Lord as *the Rock eternal*, implying He can't be shaken or moved, that He is completely dependable. If our lives are based on anything other than God, then we are standing on sinking sand, which everyone knows is a terrible foundation.

God's peace did not change my circumstances that night, but it removed the terrible feeling of being alone and hopeless. When that *perfect peace* flooded into my soul It assured me that God loved me and increased my confidence *"that in all things God works for the good to those who love Him, who have been called according to His purpose"* (Romans 8:28 NIV) God didn't reveal His plan for my life that night, but I instinctively knew that I could trust Him with my future. What an amazing God!

Grief is natural, normal, and numbing, and all of us go through it from time to time. If we know the Lord and trust His love for us, though, we should be able to say with the Psalmist, *"For his anger endureth but a moment; in his favour is life: weeping may endure for a night, but joy cometh in the morning."* (Ps. 30:5 KJV) By faith we see God working in our lives.

Whatever grief you are going through, or may go through, *"Casting all your care upon Him; for He careth for you."* (1 Peter 5:7 KJV) When we believe that God knows what we are going through and that He has prepared something better for us and we trust Him in the midst of our pain, we can experience His peace *"which transcends all understanding and will guard your hearts and minds in Christ Jesus."* (Philippians 4:7 NIV)

Week 57

Can I Do You a Favor?

WHILE PUMPING GAS INTO my pickup one Saturday morning, I overheard an argument on the other side of pump island. A small, female attendant couldn't get a large, drunk man to pay his full bill and he was giving her a hard time.

"I'm sorry," she explained to him in a desperate, pleading voice, "but you'll have to pay the full amount."

"No," he answered. "Besides, I'm a dollar short."

Their conversation continued like this until, feeling sorry for the attendant, I interrupted them and volunteered, "I'll pay the extra dollar."

Relieved, the girl grabbed my dollar and disappeared back into the station. The man, who looked rough and tough, smiled and thanked me. Then, almost in a stupor, he promised, "I'll pay you back if I ever see you again."

Not sure I ever wanted to see him again, I answered, "That's all right. I just wanted to help."

Turning reflective on me, he shifted gears. "Say, that's real nice. Maybe I can do you a favor or something." Then, becoming serious, he smiled a crooked grin and told me, "Maybe there's someone I can beat up for you."

By the looks of him, it appeared he could do that easily enough, but I declined the offer. Obviously, it wouldn't look good for a pastor to have a thug beating up people for him.

We started to depart when a lightbulb seemed to go on in his head. "Say, Mister. Do you get gas here on Saturdays often?" Seeing he was looking for a free hand-out, I answered, "No, not very often." With that we parted company and I never saw him again.

My gift only amounted to a dollar and I'll never receive repayment here on this earth, but I still see it as an investment in eternity. Normally, we're willing to lend to friends or people who will repay, but seldom will we give to those who we suspect either can't or won't repay. We judge that kind of giving as foolish.

Jesus Christ tells us, though, that He rewards the giver who extends help to those who are unlikely to repay. He asks some probing questions on this subject in Luke 6:32-36:

> "If you love those who love you, what credit is that to you? Even 'sinners' love those who love them. And if you do good to those who are good to you, what credit is that to you? Even 'sinners' do that. And if you lend to those from whom you expect repayment, what credit is that to you? Even 'sinners' lend to 'sinners,' expecting to be repaid in full. But love your enemies, do good to them, and lend to them without expecting to get anything back. Then your reward will be great, and you will be sons of the Most High, because He is kind to the ungrateful and wicked. Be merciful, just as your Father is merciful."

Our heavenly Father is a giver! James tells us, "*Do not be deceived, my dear brothers and sisters. Every good and perfect gift is from above, coming down from the Father of lights, who does not change like shifting shadows.*" (James 1:16, 17) God gives us everything we need for life in this world and we are dependent on Him whether we realize it or not.

Thankfully, God gives us more than we deserve. The Bible tells us, "*For God loved the world in this way: He gave His one and only Son, so that everyone who believes in Him will not perish but have eternal life.*" (Jn. 3:16) Jesus Christ is the greatest gift that anyone can receive because He alone meets our true needs in this world and in the next. God owed us nothing, and there was no way we could repay Him, but He willingly and lovingly gave His Son Jesus for us. If we understand the enormity of the Gift, the only natural response to God's love is to love Him back.

One of the ways we show our love to God is by giving back to Him a portion of what He has given us. This may be an offering to His work in the church or a gift to someone needy in His Name. When we give in God's Name, God gets the glory because we have become just like Him, someone who gives.

Week 58

Nothing is Impossible

IN OCTOBER OF 1933, twenty-year old Newt Rasor sat in a wooden chair waiting for the Copalis Beach school commissioner's decision on his request to use the school for a weekly Sunday School class. The previous Sunday Newt's pastor in nearby Aberdeen challenged everyone to do something for Christ and not just sit there in church, which is why Newt sat before the school commissioners waiting for their answer.

One of the commissioners spoke for the others when he told Newt, "There will be a Sunday School in this school over my dead body!" Dejected, but still hopeful, young Newt realized that if there was going to be an outreach in Copalis Beach, it would take a miracle.

What Newt didn't know was that God had gone before him and prepared the miracle, which was fourteen-year old Evelyn Burlingame. Evelyn's family had moved from Aberdeen to Copalis Beach that summer and she was disappointed that there was no Sunday School to attend, so she started praying, asking God to provide a place for her to worship and learn about God.

A week after Newt's rejection, he received word that the "over my dead body" commissioner had died unexpectedly that week. Sensing God's hand in the situation, he attended the next school commissioner's meeting to resubmit his request and, to his delight and God's glory, the other commissioners were now more than happy to allow a Sunday School class in the school on Sunday mornings.

Young Evelyn Burlingame witnessed first-hand the power of God, seeing that "nothing is impossible with God." Her prayers not only helped start the Sunday School, but, the following year, a regular church service was added. Several years later she would meet her future husband, a new teacher at nearby Ocean City, when he attended church in Copalis Beach. Even though she and her husband moved to Union Gap, Washington, in the1950's, she continued to support Copalis Community Church financially, and with her prayers her whole life.

Newt faithfully pastored the small church at Copalis Beach through the depression and WW II years. In the early 1950's he met young Margaret Sealy at a Bible camp in Grayland, Washington. They fell in love and married after a year of courtship and the small church really took off when the new town of Ocean Shores was established nearby in the early 60's. To accommodate the growing congregation, a beautiful new church was built in 1967.

Newt and Margaret raised 5 children and enjoyed over 50 years of marriage in Copalis Beach. Together, they impacted 3 generations of North Beach families the 59 years Newt pastored there. 100's of men, women and children were led to Jesus Christ during their ministry there and their legacy lives on among the many people who are faithfully serving Jesus with their lives. One of Newt's favorite sayings was, "You can't out give God," and he was living proof of that.

I (Jim Richards) began attending Copalis Community Church in 1978, after moving there in the spring of that year. In the fall of 1979, I received a call from God to serve Him in the ministry and left Copalis Beach in January of 1980 to minister with Village Missions for twelve years. In January of 1992, Newt called and asked me to follow in his footsteps, which I did, becoming the second pastor at Copalis Community Church in June of 1992. Newt is with the Lord now, but in October of this year (2019) the church he started celebrated eighty-six years of ministry in Copalis Beach. Even though Copalis

Beach has experienced hardships and is now just a wide place in the road, God continues to bless the church with His presence in people's lives there.

In 1966, the church faced financial hardships and was tempted to take a loan to finish building the new sanctuary. Newt was driving to Lake Quinault one afternoon when the Lord spoke to him, promising, "Open thy mouth wide, and I will fill it." (Psalm 81:10) Newt continued "opening his mouth", preaching the Word, and God faithfully provided for the church's needs up until the present time. We do not proclaim ourselves, but Jesus Christ who died, was buried, and rose again to redeem a people for Himself. We proclaim that nothing is impossible with God and we live to exalt Him. He is worthy!

Week 59

Send the Light

THE DARKNESS IN THE prison cafeteria exposed my vulnerability. As the prison chaplain I ate dinner with the guards and inmates on the night of my service at the Northern Idaho Correctional Institute. A sudden power failure left us in total darkness, transforming the prisoners from quiet and controlled to noisy and threatening in a matter of moments. Fear crept into my mind when I envisioned what could happen in the dark.

Almost immediately, the officer in charge called on his radio, "We need a flashlight in the chow hall." Then he added, "The emergency lights failed when the power went out and we're sitting here in the dark."

A few moments later a small shaft of light flooded the room when another officer walked into the cafeteria with a powerful flashlight. Seeing the light, the inmates immediately quieted down and I gained a new awareness of the security that light brings.

Jesus told His followers in Mathew 5:14, "You are the light of the world." This statement reveals two truths about our world.

First, the world exists in darkness. Apart from Jesus Christ, people are lost in the darkness of sin with its destiny of death and destruction. Whether people admit it or not, this world is dark.

Second, Christians are the only light of the world. Because Jesus Christ lives in them, they alone can expose the fruits of darkness and lead people to the safety of the Light, which is Jesus Christ. Christians are the "light of the world" because Jesus "the light of life" lives in them. Living the Christian life responsibly means not hiding our light. Jesus says, "Neither do people light a lamp and put it under a bowl. Instead, they put it on its stand, and it gives light to everyone in the house." We are the world's only hope to see the Light, so we cannot put our light under a bowl.

How do Christians "put their light under a bowl"? The key is the under. When we are unloving, unkind, unthoughtful, unforgiving, unwise, unfaithful, uncontrolled, etc., we place our light under the bowl of sin and people do not see "Christ in us, the hope of glory." Sin makes us un-Christ-like, putting our light under a bowl so the world cannot see it and come to Jesus.

Instead of putting our light under a bowl, we are encouraged to put it on a stand so others can see it. This happens when we turn our bowl over and put the light on top of it, instead of under it.

Instead of unloving, we let the love of Jesus flow through us to others. Instead of unkind, Jesus produces His kindness to others through us. Instead of unthoughtful, we ask God to open our minds to new ways of putting others first in our lives. Instead of unforgiving, we are quick to forgive, because God forgave our sins through Christ Jesus. Instead of unwise, we allow God to fill our minds with the wisdom of His Scriptures. Instead of unfaithful, we demonstrate our faithfulness through our obedience to God's commands. Instead of uncontrolled, we allow the Holy Spirit to take control of our bodies and our tongues so God will be glorified through us. When we are transformed from darkness to light, our light "shines before men" and they will "praise our Father Who is in heaven."

The children's song, "This little light of mine, I'm going to let it shine, let it shine, let it shine" (Harry Dixon Loes) should convey the desire of our hearts. When it does, the glory of Christ's light will be obvious to all.

Week 60
The Whole Truth

SEVERAL YEARS AGO, when my oldest grandson Malachi was 4 years old, I talked to him on the phone. Skipping the preliminaries, he got right down to business.

"Grandpa," he started breathlessly, "I've got a new workbook."

"You do?" I responded in my most interested voice.

"Yes, I do!" he shot back, adding, "It has the word yarn in it."

"Wow!" I exclaimed, tickled by his excitement.

"And," he went on, as if sharing a secret of the universe, "yarn stars with an X!"

Okay, I thought, there seems to be a little confusion here about X's and Y's, but I don't think it's a big enough problem to address at this early stage of the game. So, for now, as far as I am concerned, yarn starts with an X!

Reflecting on this, though, I believe Malachi's confusion is similar to one that many Christians have today, and it is something we do need to be concerned about. What do I think we should be concerned about? Dr. John Mitchell, who started Multnomah Bible College in Portland, Oregon, revealed what it was every time he exposed our Biblical illiteracy. Using his best Scottish brogue, he pointed his finger at us and playfully scolded us, "You don't know your Bible!"

I think Dr. Mitchell's accusation describes much of the Church today, which shouldn't surprise us since the Apostle Paul warned his young protege Timothy that "there will be terrible times in the last

217

days." (2 Tim. 3:1) Consequently, Paul charged Timothy to "*Preach the Word*" (2 Tim. 4:2), prophesying that,

> "*the time will come when men will not put up with sound doctrine. Instead, to suit their own desires, they will gather around them a great number of teachers to say what their itching ears want to hear.*" (2 Tim. 4:3)

It's happening in our day! It seems that too many messages today are no more than self-help seminars. Topical sermons focus on "feel good" verses that promise health and wealth, freedom and joy, power and purpose, promoting the "blessings", but ignoring everything else, including the warnings and commandments. Like eating donuts, topical messages can be good every now and then, but if that's all we're eating we will be dangerously malnourished spiritually.

Before someone protests, consider what Dr. Emerson Eggerich, in his excellent seminar "Love and Respect", (video: GraceAgMedia, Feb. 10, 2020, https://www.youtube.com/watch?v=yDXKnOTN8Vc) said about truth: "Our courts insist on the 'whole truth' because they recognized long ago that part of the 'truth' can be a lie."

I think Paul says the same thing when he tells us, "*Do your best to present yourself to God as one approved, a workman who does not need to be ashamed and who correctly handles the Word of truth.*" (2 Tim. 2:15) The whole truth, and nothing but the truth, should be our motto during these dangerous "last days."

Yes, we need encouraging messages, but we also need the "full armor of God" (Eph. 6:13) to "take our stand against the devil's schemes." (Eph. 6:13) I believe we should be working through whole books of the Bible for this to happen, studying them verse by verse, passage by passage, book by book, to discover what God is saying to us in His Word.

I have been studying and preaching God's Word for almost forty years and Dr. Mitchell's assessment of my spiritual condition seems truer today than it did back then. The more I plumb the depths of God's Word, the more I recognize the shallowness of my knowledge of Him and His ways. It seems that the closer I get to Him, the farther I have to go!

I have been overjoyed to see some in the church who have unknowingly encouraged me by their love for the Word. When you see them listening to the Word, reading the Word, memorizing the Word, and meditating on the Word, you know God is doing a deep work in their hearts. Their spiritual growth and vitality challenges me to stay committed to the whole Word of God.

Week 61
An Epidemic

IT HAS BECOME ALL TOO frequent in our society. Twice this last week we witnessed carnage in two of our cities, where a lone gunman killed and injured dozens of people. It's tragic, it's sad, it's unsettling and it causes us to wonder, "Why? Why is this happening?"

Many are quick to point fingers to explain the cause of this national pandemic of violence. The standard knee jerk response of many is, "It's the guns!" They reason, if there were more laws concerning firearms, there would be fewer deaths. The problem with this line of thinking is that the people who commit these crimes aren't concerned about laws, as witnessed by the shooting deaths in Chicago, which has some of the toughest gun laws in America. It's my own opinion, but I think if more good people carried guns, less bad people would be willing to risk their lives attacking others.

Some point their fingers at our President. "If he wasn't so divisive", they argue, "impressionable people wouldn't go to such violent extremes." It seems to me that this is just an underhanded scheme to kill dissent in our country. They are essentially saying, "You are a bad person if you don't agree with me." The outcome of this line of thinking will be the suspension of our First Amendment rights, which guarantees the freedom of speech, including the right to disagree with those who somehow think differently than they do.

A few even blame supporters of the President for the breakdowns in our society. Their hatred of the President is so intense that they label half of the country who voted for the President as racists and haters. I fear that rhetoric like this is so corrosive and divisive that we will not be able to function together peacefully.

It seems strange to me that few are linking the violence and self-destruction to the decline of religious values in our society. As a nation, we no longer give our young people the benefit of religious training, declaring what God says is right and wrong. Instead of providing them with a proven pathway to follow, we throw them into the tempest of life without the Compass to navigate the perilous currents they encounter. We shout, "Goodluck!", throw them overboard, and, then, watch them wander and wallow trying to gain their bearings. Many never do.

Romans 1 is the most accurate assessment of our country's condition:

> "The wrath of God is being revealed from heaven against all the godlessness and wickedness of men who suppress the truth by their wickedness." (Rom. 1:18)

When we reject God, we become "fools" and "God gives (us) over to the sinful desires of (our) hearts." (Rom. 1:24) The worst thing that can happen to any person or country is for God to give them over to their sinful desires, which always leads to destruction.

The Bible warns us that this will happen in the end times. 2 Timothy 3 tells us,

> "But mark this: there will be terrible times in the last days. People will be lovers of themselves, lovers of money, boastful, proud, abusive, disobedient to their parents, ungrateful, unholy, without love, unforgiving, slanderous, without self-control, brutal, not lovers of the good, treacherous, rash, conceited, lovers of pleasure rather that lovers of God."

It doesn't take an astute mind to look around and see that this is a pretty good description of our society. It is here and it is sad.

How do we combat this peril that threatens us and our children? Our only recourse is what Paul reveals in 2 Timothy 3:16-17:

"All Scripture is God-breathed and is useful for teaching, rebuking, correcting and training in righteousness, so that the man of God may be thoroughly equipped for every good work."

God's Word, not laws, higher education, human traditions, rules or regulations, can equip us for this maze we call life. When the Spirit of God instills the Word of God deep in our souls, then we are equipped to handle the treacherous currents of life in this world.

We need to read our Bibles, asking the Spirit of God to open the eyes of our understanding. When we search the Scriptures for life's answers and train our children to live by the precepts in God's Word, God has the opportunity to work in our lives, preparing us for works of service that will save us and others, stemming the flood of destruction that has been unleashed on our land.

If we will give God first place in our lives and land, He will guide us through this wilderness we call life in a way that is safe, secure and satisfying.

Week 62

Downhill Racer

FIFTY YEARS LATER, my first skiing experience remains vivid in my mind. Standing on top of what I mistook for the bunny run at Crystal Mountain, I peered over the precipice before me. As my pre-skiing excitement drained into the snow beneath my wooden skis, I couldn't help but wonder, "How in the world am I going to get down this hill alive?"

Just then a young boy came to the top of the rope tow. Sporting a racing helmet and numbers, he turned, crouched and sped straight down the hill. Watching in amazement, I thought, "So that's how you do it." Then I reasoned to myself, "If he can do it, so can I!"

With my new-found courage, I chose an angle to the side of the hill and pushed off with my poles. I descended slowly, balancing precariously, but quickly picked up speed. Worried about falling, I remembered the young racers crouch, so I bent my knees like he did. "Funny," I thought to myself, "this seems to make me go faster."

I didn't have time to ponder this new discovery long, though, because my bleary eyes spotted a snowbank directly in front of me at the bottom of the hill. Unable to stop or turn, I hit the snowbank at full speed (what felt like a hundred miles per hour) and shot forward like a ball out of a cannon. Flying through the air, I moaned to myself, "Oh no!" as I plowed face first into the snow.

I laid there a second, mentally checking my limbs to see if they were still attached, which they were, and then stood up. Looking down at my skis, I saw they had broken off in front of my too tight bindings. There was nothing I could do but walk back to the lodge, rent a new pair of skis, and start over on a gentler slope.

Looking back, I recognize my mistakes. Someone knowledgeable should have adjusted my bindings; I should have asked for directions to the bunny hill; and a ski lesson would have certainly helped. Of course, when you think you already know everything, you don't do those things and you end up paying the consequences for your bad choices. Fortunately, that day, I had the opportunity to start over and do things right. It was a lot more fun in the long run.

Life is much like skiing. Often, we think that we're downhill racers right from the start. In our pride and cockiness, we start straight down the course thinking we'll take care of the problems as they crop up. Usually, we've overestimated our own ability and underestimated the potential problems we'll face. In our pride we completely ignore God, who said "Pride goes before destruction, a haughty spirit before a fall." (Proverbs 16:18) and "God opposes the proud." (James 2:6) If the obstacles in front of us were not cause for caution and alarm, the thought of God opposing us should bring us back to our right minds.

On top of the obstacles we face in our life journey, there's also a snowbank at the bottom of the course called death, which none of us can successfully traverse on our own. The Bible warns us that we will all stand before God, our Creator, and give an account of our lives. He won't be asking if we had a good time down here and every action, word, thought and motive will be exposed.

That's why God has given us His Word, the Bible, and His Holy Spirit. The Bible is life's textbook and the Holy Spirit is life's instructor. 2 Timothy 3:16,17 tells us, *"All Scripture is God-breathed and is useful for teaching, rebuking, correcting and training in righteousness, so that the man of God may be thoroughly equipped for every good work."*

God wants to train us to be experts in this journey we call life and He does wonderful things for all who call upon Him. When we allow

Him to have control of our lives, it's amazing how many crashes we avoid and how exciting the journey it. It's the only way to go!

Week 63
Choices

CHOICES: THEY MAKE or break us. We make choices, big and little, every day of our lives. Sometimes choices impact our lives very little; other times a single choice changes the direction of our life. Big or little, good choices bring blessings and bad choices bring curses. More than any other factor, our choices determine who we are, what we are doing, and where we are going in life.

Joshua was a man who made good choices in his life. As Moses's trusted aide and, later, as leader of the Israelite army that conquered Palestine, he always made the right decision. It isn't surprising that his last message as leader to the Israelite people involved choices. He challenged the Israelite's: *"Choose for yourselves this day whom you will serve,"* (Joshua 24:15) Joshua's challenge tells us three things we need to understand about our choices.

First, we can't delegate our choices to someone else. He says, "Choose for <u>yourself</u>". Often, we allow family, friends, church, or circumstances to dictate vital spiritual choices for us. When blessings or curses, heaven or hell are the outcome, though, we can't afford to trust that decision to others. God gave us His Word, the Bible, to direct each of us to the Truth, Jesus Christ. We alone are accountable before God, so we can't allow someone else to make life or death choices for us.

Second, we can't procrastinate with our choices. "Choose for yourselves <u>this day</u>". It's easy to put off important choices. We'll do it tomorrow, or next week, or when we get older. Unfortunately, tomorrow never comes; next week is always just around the corner; and we seem to forget what it was we were going to decide when old age sneaks up on us and surprises us. The longer we wait to decide for God, the harder the decision becomes. That's why the writer to the Hebrews counsels us, *"Today, if you hear His voice, do not harden your hearts as you did in the rebellion."* (Hebrews 3:15) Our hearts get hard, calloused and unresponsive to the Holy Spirit the longer we put off our decision. "Today" is the day of salvation if the Lord is speaking to your hearts. The decision is too important to put off.

Third, don't mistake the choice we're making. *"Choose for yourselves this day whom you will serve."* The Bible clearly teaches that we either serve God or Satan – there is no other choice, whether we believe that or not. Here's where we protest, "But I am a good person!" That may or may not be true, but the issue is, who are you serving, not are you nice or not. If you were hired to do a job and were later fired because you didn't do the work the company asked you to do, it wouldn't matter if you claimed to be nice or not. In the same way, we were created to serve and glorify our God. We serve God by loving Him and obeying His commands. On the other hand, we serve Satan by loving self and obeying our human cravings. The truth is, we 're all born into slavery to sin and the only hope we have for true freedom is to surrender our lives to Jesus Christ, *"Who died to redeem us from the curse of the Law"* (Gal. 3:13) and bring us into the glorious Kingdom of God.

Our pride tells us we are no one's servant, which is one of Satan's greatest deceptions. John Wimber, who played for the Righteous Brothers and later started the Vineyard Churches, told a story about an experience he had before he chose Jesus Christ to be his Lord and Savior.

John was walking down a street in Hollywood when he approached a man wearing a sandwich board that read - "I'm a fool for Jesus Christ." As John walked by the man, he thought to himself, "You sure are!" After passing the man, though, he turned around and saw a different message on the back of the sandwich board that read - "Whose fool are you?"

Jesus said, "No servant can serve two masters. Either he will hate the one and love the other, or he will be devoted to the one and despise the other. You cannot serve both God and Money." The Pharisees, who loved money, heard all this and were sneering at Jesus. He said to them, *"You are the ones who justify yourselves in the eyes of men, but God knows your hearts. What is highly valued among men is detestable in God's sight."* (Luke16:13-15)

The choice of whom we will serve determines our future for eternity, so let's make the choice Joshua did. He declared to Israel and us, *"As for me and my household, we will serve the Lord."* (Joshua 24:15) What a great choice!

Week 64

Doing or Done?

DOING AND DONE ARE natural opposites. It is impossible to be both doing and done at the same time. If someone is still doing, he can't be done and if they are done, they can't still be doing. Because of this fact, the "doing or done" test points out the difference between true Christianity and every false religion.

Paul reveals this test in Romans 10:3-4. After sharing his burden for the Jews and acknowledging their zeal for God, he says:

> *"Since they did not know the righteousness that comes from God and sought to establish their own, they did not submit to God's righteousness. Christ is the end of the law, so that there may be righteousness for everyone who believes."*

Every false religion tries to establish a righteousness of its own. Individuals work hard to satisfy what they believe are requirements for eternal life. Different terms may be used in different religions, but they are all basically saying the same thing – there is something you must "do" to have eternal life; they are still stuck in the "doing" trap.

Romans 3:23 points out the futility of their hard work to attain salvation when it says, *"For all have sinned and fall short of the glory of God."* No matter how hard they work at their religion, their "doing" is destined to "fall short", since their "doing "can never satisfy God's demand of complete holiness.

True Christianity, on the other hand, realizes man's inability to satisfy God's righteous requirements. Instead to trying to establish a righteousness of their own, the Christian puts his or her faith in the righteousness of Christ. Realizing their utter inability to satisfy God' standard for salvation, they voluntarily give themselves to Christ in faith, believing He is the only way. Believing that the penalty for sin has already been paid in full, or "done", by Jesus on the cross, they quit trying to justify themselves before God and give themselves wholeheartedly to Jesus out of thanksgiving for what He "did" for them on the Cross. Jesus is the end of the Law for every believer.

Are you caught up in the futility of trying to do something to satisfy God for your salvation? Is so, Jesus counsels you, *"Come to me, all you who are weary and burdened, and I will give you rest."* (Mt. 11:28)

Week 65

How Much?

WHEN ONE OF MY BOYS was ten, he earned ten dollars mowing a lady's yard. He received his payment and, then, wondered if he should give some of it to God. After I explained the principle of tithing, he cautiously asked, "How much should I give?"

When I told him that tithing in the Bible was giving 10% of your earnings to the Lord, I could see the gears in his mind crunching the data until, finally, he asked, "Does ten percent of ten dollars mean I give ten cents to God?"

After correcting his math, I watched him wrestle with the enormity of the sacrifice. Finally, convinced that it was the right thing to do, he announced, "One dollar isn't enough. I'm going to put two dollars in the offering on Sunday!"

Then a new thought entered his mind. "Am I supposed to tithe on the eight dollars that is left the next week?" he asked. Clearly, by projecting this principle into the future, he envisioned his money dwindling week by week until finally there would be nothing left for him. For a ten-year-old, this was incentive enough to spend the rest as quickly as possible. When I explained that we are only asked to give on our earnings once, his concern drained away and was replaced by a determination to do what he believed was right.

The principle of tithing is tough to handle for many Christians. Why does God ask us to tithe, we wonder? Here are several reasons.

First, by tithing we give God thanks for what He has supplied us. It acknowledges that everything we have is a gift from Him.

Second, our tithe declares our dependence on Him. By giving to God we declare our trust in Him supplying our needs.

Third, our tithe pledges our support for His work on earth. Through our sharing, we enter into God's work of bringing people to Christ.

Fourth, we are obedient to God by fulfilling one of His commands.

Fifth, we demonstrate our faith in God. Giving proves our sincerity in worshipping Him.

Last, we open the door for God's blessing in our lives. Our obedience gives God the freedom to pour out His blessing in every area of our lives. Countless thousands of people have testified to the blessings of giving to God. My predecessor, Newt Rasor, loved to say, "You can't out give God!"

Some may protest, "But I can't afford to give." This brings up the question, is my inability to give a result of my poverty, or is my poverty the result of not giving? Each individual has to ask and answer this question themselves.

God makes this statement in Malachi 3:8-10:

> *"Will a man rob God? Yet you rob me. But you ask, 'How do we rob You?' In tithes and offerings. You are under a curse – the whole nation of you – because you are robbing me. Bring the whole tithe into the storehouse, that there may be food in My house. Test me in this, says the Lord Almighty, and see if I will not throw open the floodgates of heaven and pour out so much blessing that you will not have room enough for it."*

I go back to my son's question – "How much should I give?" In the Old Testament the Law required ten percent. Now, though, since Jesus Christ fulfilled the requirements of the Law for us, there is no set figure we should give. In the New Testament, when the Apostle Paul was collecting an offering for the saints in Jerusalem, he advised the Corinthians,

> "*Remember this: whoever sows sparingly will also reap sparingly, and whoever sows generously will also reap generously. Each man should give what he has decided in his heart to give, not reluctantly or under compulsion, for God loves a cheerful giver. And God is able to make all grace abound to you, so that in all things at all times, having all that you need, you will abound in every good work.*"

Then he adds, "*You will be made rich in every way so that you can be generous on every occasion, and through us your generosity will result in thanksgiving to God.*" (2 Cor. 9:6-8;11)

So, there is no set figure in the New Testament. One dollar may be a great sacrifice for someone while ninety percent may be nothing to someone else. The key issue is: "God loves a cheerful giver."

Week 66

Infant or Infinite?

WHEN MY SECOND SON John was a year-old, we traveled to Grandma's house for a visit. Of course, Grandma was excited to see her 'big boy' and showered him with love. While they were hugging my wife commented, "Aren't little boys nice, Grandma?" We were surprised when she answered, "Yes, but it's too bad they grow up to be hairy old men!"

Basically, she was saying, "The child is cute and submissive, but the adult version can be coarse and demanding."

Some people regard Jesus Christ this way. They just love the little baby boy in the manger, who is cute and cuddly – and non-threatening! We can come to the manger to marvel and coo with our baby sounds – and leave when we want to.

Yes, it's easy to handle a baby Jesus laying in the straw, but what about the grownup Jesus? What about the Jesus who is Lord of Glory? What about the Jesus who said, *"If anyone would come after me, he must deny himself and take up his cross and follow me."* (Lk. 9:23)?

"Well, ahem, uh, that's another matter," we say. We like the baby Jesus model, but we're not so sure about the grownup Jesus who demands worship.

Friends, we can't have one without the other. The baby Jesus in the manger was just as much King of the universe as the Jesus who now sits at the right hand of the Father on His throne in Glory. Philippians 2:6-11 explains why Jesus left heaven to come to earth as a baby:

"Who being in very nature God, did not consider equality with God something to grasped, but made himself nothing, taking the very nature of a servant, being made in human likeness. And being found in appearance as a man, he humbled himself and became obedient to death – even death on a cross! Therefore, God exalted him to the highest place and gave him the name that is above every name, that at the name of Jesus every knee should bow, in heaven and on earth, and every tongue confess that Jesus Christ is Lord, to the glory of God the Father."

King Herod recognized the danger the baby Jesus represented, knowing he would grow up to become a king. Jesus threatened Herod's self-centered delusions of control of his life, so he tried to eliminate Jesus and ordered the killing of all the baby boys in Bethlehem. All he succeeded in doing was bringing condemnation on himself and sealing his fate in Hell. Jesus is the King of glory and nothing can undermine His rule.

Today people love celebrating the birth of Jesus, but they resent any attempt to make him Lord of their lives. Whether they admit it or not, they have no room for Jesus. In John 19:15, when Pilate asked the crowd, *"Shall I crucify your king?"* and they answered, *"We have no king but Caesar,"* they expressed what most people believe today. The world does not want Jesus to be their King and foolishly fights against him. Imagine the world's reaction when Jesus returns as the conquering King to claim His rightful role as Creator of the universe.

As we think about the birth of Jesus, we need to be like the Wisemen who *"bowed down and worshiped him."* (Mt. 2:10) Even today, that is the only appropriate response when in the presence of the King. So, this Christmas, worship Jesus and give him the gift of yourself.

Week 67

Take a Walk

WE'VE ALL SEEN IT HAPPEN. A man and woman fall in love. They have a family. They get involved in their community or church. They establish themselves in their work. They purchase a home and everything that goes with it.

And, then, suddenly, they break up. We hear words like, "I don't love you anymore," or, "I never really knew you," or, "Our lives have gone in different directions." It's a sad, but true, fact that the second highest divorce rate in our country is among couples who have been married twenty years or more.

How does it happen? Why do two people who have shared their lives with each other for so long come to a place where they can no longer live together? Well, first of all, it doesn't happen overnight. It is a process that has involved many years.

What happens is that two people who have lived together gradually become strangers to each other. They get so caught up in their relationship with their kids, or their friends, or their job, or their activities, or their dreams, that their relationship with each other slowly dies.

Second of all, they forget that we all have an enemy that "seeks to steal, kill and destroy." (Jn. 10:10) When God finished creation, including us, we're told, *"God saw all that he had made, and it was very good indeed."* (Gen. 1:31) Satan hates God, including all that he has

241

made, and he constantly schemes to destroy it. If we are not aware of these schemes we are easily destroyed.

So, what do we do to 'stand against the schemes of the devil?' Concerning our relationships with our spouses we need to remind ourselves of God's priorities for us. According to the Bible, our number one priority after our relationship to God and Jesus is our spouse. Your husband or wife is to be more important to you than your kids, your friends, your job, your hobbies, your possessions, and even your dreams. Instead of having a relationship that is slowly dying, God wants it to become more and more alive and exciting.

One of the greatest enemies that every couple faces today is time, or more appropriately, lack of time. The daily grind leaves us so little time to really communicate and share our lives with each other. No wonder that so many people become strangers to each other.

My wife and I face this same kind of pressure. Many couples go days, weeks, months, even years, without really communicating with each other, sharing their inner thoughts, desires, fears, and dreams. Studies show that the average couple communicates with each other less than two minutes a day. Even when we want to communicate with each other we're often fighting a losing battle because of the distractions of everyday living.

How can we win this battle to keep the communication lines open for growing and exciting relationships? First, we acknowledge the truth of that old adage, "Failure to plan is planning to fail." We have to plan to make time for each other.

We do this several ways. Sometimes it is a walk together on the beach. We have a favorite log that we stop to sit on so we can talk and pray together. A new favorite is soaking in our hot tub together. This gives us undistracted time to talk about our day and pray together. Sometimes it is simply having coffee together after breakfast for few minutes to visit and pray. The issue isn't what we do, but how we make time for each other.

I realize that kids complicate things, but when I was younger, we would try to find some time together while they were playing or after the they went to bed. As much as possible we should make time for each other without the distraction of children and their constant needs. Not only is that time important for us, but it is for them, also.

Not only do we need to make time for each other, but we also need to make time for God. God is able to do the impossible in our lives, but He needs our cooperation to do the necessary work in us. It is important that we humble ourselves before Him, asking Him to renew our marriages and relationships. He loves to reignite the spark that made our marriages exciting.

Finally, if you want an exciting, vibrant marriage, take time to pray together. Ask God to bless your spouse; invite Him to examine your heart to see if there is any offensive way in you; give Him permission to change you; tell Him you want Him to be glorified in your marriage. God loves to show Himself strong in our lives when we draw near to Him.

May God be glorified in your marriage!

Week 68

Through the Screen Door

CREATION MIRRORS GOD, the Creator. Consequently, God reveals Himself to us through the natural things He has made. During Christ's ministry on earth He often used natural illustrations to teach spiritual applications. Today, with a sensitivity to the Holy Spirit, we can comprehend spiritual truths through natural examples, too.

One good example of this truth involved a bum lamb I had in Montana. I herded our milking goats and the lamb onto our front lawn where they grazed on the fresh green grass. As I watched them, our phone rang in our mobile home, so I quickly jumped up the metal grate stairs, pushed open the screen door and slammed it shut as I dashed for the phone.

After saying a breathless "Hello" on the phone, I heard a tremendous crash behind me. Startled, I turned around and was greeted by a worried "Baa" from our lamb, who was standing in our kitchen in front of the screen door, which no longer had a screen in it.

When I ran for the phone, the lamb sensed danger and took off after me. After I ran through the screen door, the lamb did, too. Unfortunately, the screen door was closed when the lamb got there, so she just ran through it. Despite the damage to the screen door, we couldn't get mad at the lamb because it just did what it was programed to do – follow the shepherd!

My episode pointed out the truth that sheep are followers. The Bible compares us to sheep, because just like them, we are followers, too. The problem isn't that we are followers, though, but that we follow the wrong shepherds. Isaiah graphically depicts our true condition when he says, *"All we, like sheep have gone astray."* (Is. 53:6) Instead of following the Good Shepherd, Jesus Christ, we follow the crowd, fulfilling our natural desires, and end up going astray. Instead of being led into green pastures we find ourselves grazing in the weeds of life.

Whether we admit it or not, we've all gone astray and become easy prey for our *"enemy the devil (who) prowls around like a roaring lion looking for someone to devour"*. (1 Peter 5:8)

Whether we realize it or not, we all need a Shepherd and the only One qualified for the job is the Good Shepherd, Jesus Christ. Jesus alone knows where the green pastures are; He alone is strong enough to protect us from the ravenous wolves; He alone is willing to lay down His life for His sheep.

Jesus gave His life for us, the sheep of His pasture; He lived among us and knows the dangers we face and is strong enough to protect us; He faced our great enemy, Death, and overcame it though His resurrection, offering eternal life for all who follow Him; He alone is qualified to be our Shepherd.

Jesus tells us, *"I am the good Shepherd. The good Shepherd lays down his life for the sheep."* As a result, *"His sheep follow Him because they know His voice."* (John 10:11, 14) We follow the Good Shepherd because we have heard His voice.

A good friend of mine interrupted a cult member who was witnessing to him and asked, "Did you say you would die for me?" The cult member answered, "No, I didn't say that." and then continued witnessing to my friend. My friend interrupted him again and asked the same question, "Did you say you would die for me?" Somewhat annoyed, the cult member answered, "No, I didn't say I would die for you." My friend ended the conversation by telling the cult member, "That's right. The only one who loves me enough to die for me is Jesus and I'm following Him."

Who are you following today? If not the Good Shepherd, why not? If not now, when? Listen to the Good Shepherd's voice and believe that He is the only One worth following in life. He alone can lead you into green pastures where there is abundance and safety. He alone was willing to lay down His life to protect you. Let Him become the Shepherd of your soul and follow Him with joy, because He loves you.

Week 69

Broken Arrows

HUNTING SEASON IS JUST around the corner and the adrenaline is beginning to pump in many of us. That trophy buck somehow escaped us last year, but "he won't be so lucky this year," we promise ourselves.

Several years ago, while living in Montana, I had a strong case of 'Buck Fever'. Anxious to start hunting, I borrowed a friend's bow and arrows to take advantage of the early season for bow hunters. The only condition for using my friend's bow and arrows was I would have to pay for any of the ten arrows I lost or broke. "No sweat!" I thought to myself.

Visions of Robin Hood and William Tell flooded my mind as I dreamed of filling our freezer with fresh venison. Success, of course, depended on practice, and lots of it. I stacked up four straw bales on the bank of the neighboring Butte Creek and attached a white paper plate as a target. With my admiring four-year old son, Jeremy, watching, I paced off forty steps for the proper distance, fitted the arrow in place, pulled the bowstring back, took aim, and fired.

"Ow!" I cried. The bloodthirsty bowstring had hit my elbow and left a blue bruise where there had once been a smooth, white elbow. Not easily discouraged though, I moved my elbow out of reach of the bowstring and continued my practice to the tune of "thwang" and "thump". No doubt about it, hope was running high in this 'Great White Hunter'.

As time wore on, proficiency slowly snuck in and holes could actually be seen in the white paper plate target. If the bucks in the hills were watching, they were undoubtedly quivering in their hooves as the arrows sank into the straw bales with deadly precision.

That's when it happened. Nine arrows found their target, but one flew over the bales and landed in nearby Butte Creek. Well, Christ left the ninety and nine safe sheep to find the one lost sheep, so I knew my duty. I put my bow down, told Jeremy to wait there for me, and headed into the bone-dry Butte Creek to search for the lost arrow.

Strange, the voice of disaster. My four-year old helper hollered from the top the bank, "Daddy, come quick!" Worried that something had happened to Jeremy, I rushed up the bank and found him standing next to the four bales of hay, which had all fallen over. He explained, "I tried to pull an arrow out and they fell over."

I quickly pulled back the top bale and was shocked to find nine snapped arrow shafts! The arrows and my hopes for venison were both shattered, because I had missed the mark that one time.

That's often how it is in life. We have our hopes for happiness, contentment, success, peace, riches, power, etc., but invariably, we miss the mark and our hopes are squashed.

Missing the mark is one definition for sin and sin eventually shatters our lives. Romans 3:23 tells us, *"for all have sinned and fallen short of the glory of God"* and Romans 6:23 gives us the result of our poor aim, *"For the wages of sin is death"* (eternal separation from God).

We may protest, "But I only missed once!", but, like yeast that works through the whole batch of dough, sin affects every area of our lives. Vegas may claim "that whatever happens in Vegas stays in Vegas", *but the Bible says, "be sure your sins will find you out."* (Numbers 32:23)

Is it possible that even now you are suffering the consequences of missing the mark in your life? Is there brokenness in your life? Are you experiencing regret for something you've done? If so, I have good news for you.

Isaiah prophesied that Jesus came to heal up the brokenhearted (Isaiah 61:1). David tells us that, *"He heals the brokenhearted and binds up their wounds."* (Psalm 147:3} and *"The Lord is close to the brokenhearted and saves those who are crushed in spirit."* (Psalms 34:18)

No matter what we have done in our past, if we confess our sins and repent of them, the Lord is ready to forgive and restore. Jesus did not come into the world to condemn, but to save us.

King David illustrates this truth for us. After Nathan the prophet confronted David about his sin with Bathsheba and her husband Uriah, David confesses his sin – *"Against you, you only, have I sinned and done what is evil in your sight: so, you are right in your verdict and justified when you judge."* (Psalm 51:4) After confessing, David asks God to *"create in me a pure heart & renew a right spirit within me"* (Psalm 51:10) David was not only forgiven, he was restored.

In the same way, when we will confess our sins to the Lord, He loves to restore to us the joy of our His salvation.

Week 70

A Little Fixin'?

THE DAY OF RECKONING had arrived for my dad. After years of suffering with gum disease and loose teeth he was going to the dentist to have all of his teeth removed. He had put it off for a long time, but it was now out with the old and in with the new.

The dentist pulled his teeth and fitted him with new dentures, but he had to wait a week for the new dentures to arrive. Being a gummer at the age of forty is a bummer, so it was a happy day when the new chompers arrived. Unfortunately, the new dentures didn't fit right and they irritated his mouth, so he would have to make a return visit to the dentist.

That's when my mom entered the picture and decided to be the heroine. Instead of sending my dad on a long and expensive trip back to the dentist, she figured she could do a little fixin' of her own with a home remedy. Her idea was to soften the dentures a little in the oven, then put them in my dad's mouth, exert a little pressure and form fit them to his gums.

After talking my dad into her little scheme, she heated the oven up to 350 degrees, placed the dentures on a cookie sheet, put them in the oven and turned the timer on for one minute. If they looked soft enough after a minute, she would give them a second or two to cool and then place them in my dad's mouth. If everything went according to plan, my dad would have perfectly fitted dentures. Hurray!

It's really too bad that my dad's false teeth melted in the oven. If my mom's experiment had worked, she could have patented the process and gone into business for herself. As it was, my dad was still a gummer while he waited for the **new,** new false teeth to arrive to replace the **old,** new false teeth that turned into a gob of plastic in my mom's oven.

As silly as it seems, mankind employs my mom's strategy to fix our souls. We gradually become aware that the sin in our lives doesn't measure up to God's standard, leaving us with pain, guilt and shame. Somehow, though, we figure that with a little fixin' up, we can make ourselves as good as new again. We resolve to do better, discipline ourselves, work hard, and even ask God, if we are desperate, to help us fix things. In theory this sounds good, but in practice it never quite works, no matter how hard we try. Jeremiah explains why our efforts to fix the sinful heart never work. He says in Jeremiah 17:9, *"The heart is deceitful above all things and **beyond cure**. Who can understand it?"*

A little fixin' can never cure a sick, sinful, deceitful heart. Our hearts are so sick with sin that the only cure that will heal us is a brand-new heart. That's why King David, after his sin was exposed by the prophet Nathan, prayed, *"Create in me a new heart, O God, and renew a steadfast spirit within me."* (Ps 51:10)

When we cry out to God and ask Him to forgive our sins in Jesus Name, He promises to give us a new heart that will love Him and His commandments. Our new heart gives us new life that rejoices in *"Christ in you, the hope of glory."* (Col. 1:21) God, who created the new heart in us, gets glory and we get life abundant and eternal!

Even as Christians, though, we often experience a hardness of heart because of our sins. What do we do to restore our hearts? David also gave us the remedy for a hard heart in Psalm 51:17 when he says, *"The sacrifices of God are a broken spirit; a broken and contrite heart, O God, you will not despise."*

When we are broken over our sin, God will not despise our confession and will heal our hearts of the sin that wants to destroy it.

John echoes David when he says, *"If we confess our sins, He is faithful and just and will forgive us our sins and purify us from all unrighteousness."* (1 John 1:9)

Are you working hard to somehow be acceptable to God? If so, it is an impossible task – it can't be done. All God is asking us to do is to give up and give ourselves completely to His Son Jesus Christ, simply believing that He is able to *"that began a good work in you will carry it on to completion"* (Phil 1:6) because Jesus already paid for those sins when He died on the cross and shed His blood for us. Jesus paid the price for both a heart transplant and a renewed heart and He willingly and lovingly offers these as a gift to all who come to Him in faith. When we receive the gift of life from Jesus, we can say with the Apostle Paul, *"Therefore, if anyone is in Christ, he is a new creation; the old has gone, the new has come!"* (2 Corinthians 5:17)

Week 71

Where is the King?

THE WISEMEN RODE THEIR camels into Jerusalem and asked, *"Where is the one who has been born the King of the Jews? We saw His star in the east and have come to worship Him."* (Mt. 2:2) Upon discovering that a king had been born in Israel, despite the distance, inconvenience and cost involved, they had traveled hundreds of miles to find Him and worship Him – it was that important to them.

Imagine their surprise when they arrived in Jerusalem and found out that they were the only ones looking for the King. It must have been a shock to realize that the King's own subjects were not interested in Him. Israel's religious leaders knew about the prophecies declaring that the King would be born in Bethlehem, but they were unwilling to travel the eight miles to search for Him, and sent the Wisemen in their place. Obviously, there were forces at work to keep the people from finding their King, the Lord Jesus Christ.

Those same forces are still at work today. If the Wisemen were to come into our shopping malls, our schools, our places of work, our homes and, even, our churches, they would still have a hard time finding someone who could direct them to Jesus. Oh, they would find Santa Claus, Christmas songs, reindeer, sleighs, a holiday spirit and a lot of other distractions, but it would be difficult to find Jesus.

It may be true that it is still difficult to find Jesus at Christmas time, but it is also true that wise men and women are still searching for Him – and finding Him. Somehow, they have tuned out the distractions of the season and concentrated on the real reason for the season, Jesus Christ the Son of God. Like all the wisemen before them who found Jesus, they have bowed down, worshipped, presented their gifts, and have been enriched by their encounter with the King. Also, like the wisemen, their lives have gone in a different direction after their encounter with the King.

Maybe you have been distracted by the traditions and celebrations and overlooked Jesus at Christmas time. In all of your hustle and bustle you've failed to search for Jesus so you could fall down in worship before Him. What must you do to find Him? It's really very simple.

Like the Wisemen before you, you have to set aside the everyday cares of this world and begin the journey to find Jesus. Jesus said, *"Seek and you will find."* (Luke 11:9) If you will just set your heart on finding Jesus, He will reveal Himself to you, and you will find Him.

When you do find Him, you will experience the joy of bending your knee before your King to worship Him, giving Him the glory that only He deserves. In exchange for your worship He will give you the gift of life, joy and peace. Unlike the other gifts we receive at Christmas, which fade and whither with time, His gifts will grow and become more and more valuable as time goes by.

In your Christmas celebration, won't you concentrate on finding Jesus? It is the only wise thing to do!

Week 72
Making Good Choices

A YOUNG WOMAN LANDED a great job as a paralegal assistant. She hadn't been doing well up until then – a messy divorce, child custody issues, overdue bills, a part-time waitress job and uncertainties about the future. Things changed for the better one day, though, when she waited on a lawyer, who hired her on the spot after discovering that she was a trained paralegal.

During her second week of work at the law firm her washing machine broke down, so she called an appliance repairman, who scheduled an appointment for the next day. She asked her new boss if she could have the day off so she could be home when the repairman came and he answered, "Well, I guess it's your choice."

She stayed home the next day, had her washing machine fixed, and enjoyed an unexpected day off.

The following morning, when she arrived at the law office for work, her boss was waiting for her at the door. He asked her, "Did you get your washing machine fixed?" and she replied, "Yes." Then he informed her, "By the way, you're fired."

Shocked, she asked him, "Why?" and he explained, "For taking the day off." "But you told me it was my choice," she objected. "It was," he responded, and, then, added, "You made the wrong one."

The consequences of her choice were devastating!

Whether we agree or disagree with the young woman's boss, most of us would admit that we constantly make choices that affect our lives.

Sadly, though, many of us are unaware of the consequences that often result from our choices. We see this all of the time. People make a bad choice and, then, they're surprised and angry about the outcome. "Life isn't fair," they complain because they can't do whatever they want to do without paying the consequences for their choice.

Whether we like it or not, we get to make the choice, but we don't get to choose the consequences of our choices.

In thinking about this the other day, it occurred to me that God is pro-choice. Before you stone me, let me explain myself. I am saying that God allows us to make our own choices. He presents us with the choice, explains the consequences of our choice, even pleads with us to make the right choice, but He won't make the choice for us. This is what theologians define as man's free will.

Before entering the Promised Land, Moses informed the Israelites that they would be faced with two choices: either obedience, which would result in blessings, or disobedience, which would result in curses. He then challenged the people who would make the choices with these words:

> "I call heaven and earth to witness against you today, that I have set before you life and death, blessing and curse. Therefore, choose life, that you and your offspring may live, loving the Lord your God, obeying His voice and holding fast to Him." (Deut. 30:19,20)

Joshua, Moses' successor, summed up this teaching succinctly when he challenged the Israelites, "Choose you this day whom you will serve." He then informed them, "But as for me and my house, we will serve the Lord." (Joshua 24:15)

Ultimately, every choice we make comes down to this – who will I serve? Choices reveal values, exposing the thoughts and intentions of the heart. When the young woman's boss said, "It's your choice," he really was saying, "I want to see if you are more concerned about our company or your yourself." Her choice revealed a lot more than she realized. So does ours.

Whether we realize it or not, our nation, which is the collective will of its citizens, is constantly making choices that affect our lives. More and more, we are choosing our own way instead of God's way and the consequences are becoming more and more devastating.

The Psalmist asks, "How can a young man keep his way pure?" The answer is, *"By guarding it according to your Word."* He then makes this commitment, *"With my whole heart I seek You; let me not wander from Your commandments! I have stored up Your Word in my heart that I might not sin against You."* (Psalm 119:9-11)

O God, help us to choose life!

Week 73

Spiners For Sail

SEVERAL YEARS AGO, a visitor came to our church who attended a Family Integrated Church (FIC) in Everett. When I asked her, "Why do you attend a family integrated church?" she surprised me by answering, "Because we wanted our sons (ages thirteen and fifteen) to be around young men, not boys."

Most churchgoers would be puzzled by her answer. Many would ask, "Doesn't she want a church with teens in it?" "What about a good youth group?" "How does she keep her sons interested in church and spiritual things?" Obviously, in our day and age, where the evangelical church loses seventy-five percent of its children to the world, these are good and appropriate questions.

That seventy-five percent number (confirmed by most surveys and common sense) is a troubling number. How can we be losing so many kids when our churches are bigger, with better music, more interesting programs and materials, and a legion of gifted, committed youth workers? If anything, we should be seeing more of our children following Jesus, not less. What's going on? Are we missing something? Can this trend be turned around?

If we want answers to these troubling questions, we need to turn to the Bible, God's inspired, definitive Word to mankind, instead of looking for man centered ideas. Too often, we look to the world, adopting its methods and adapting its programs to fit the needs of the church.

We end up like Moses, who struck the rock twice instead of speaking to it as God commanded him. Because God is gracious, Moses still got water, but he missed entering the Promised Land because of his disobedience. Just because our programs seem to work doesn't mean they'll get us to where we need to go, which is training our children to love Jesus Christ.

So, what does the Bible say about training children to be followers of Jesus Christ? God's program can be summed up with one word – fathers! That's it, we ask. Yes, that seems to be it in both the Old and New Testaments.

Fathers are commanded to be the primary teachers and trainers of their children in the home and on the road, from morning to evening (Dt. 6:1-9; Eph. 6:4) Anything that encroaches on or diminishes the father as spiritual leaders in their homes and churches ultimately undermines the work that God wants to do in their families. This doesn't mean fathers can't delegate others to help, but it does mean he has the primary responsibility.

What about the lady's comment on "young men, not teenagers"? Essentially, she was saying that she and her husband were training their boys to become men, not boys. If you want boys to become men, then they need to be influenced and trained by men, not other boys (same is true with girls becoming women). Unfortunately, when we throw our children into age segregated groups, they often become more concerned with their peers than their leader. The very programs we employ for our children's spiritual training and safety often contain dangerous elements that counteract and undermine our desires for them. Fathers, this requires wisdom!

This truth was illustrated to me a few years back by a young father who takes seriously his responsibility to train his children. He lives and works at a fish hatchery and he's passed on to his boys his love for fishing. When they were about seven and eight, the boys found some fishing spinners in the river by their home and tried selling them to local fishermen, with little success.

That next winter, they received a spinner making kit for Christmas. They made twenty-nine spinners, hoping to sell them to local fishermen. Unsuccessful the year before, they asked their dad for advice and he told them, "Set up a stand by the river, make a sign advertising your product, and, then, talk to the fishermen when they came to the banks of the river."

Later that next day, the dad looked across the fish hatchery to the river and saw a table with a sign that read, "SPINERS FOR SAIL", with several fishermen talking to his boys. An hour later, both boys came home excited because they had sold all twenty-nine spinners. They made a nice little profit and, more importantly, learned a good business lesson from their dad that is sure to bless them the rest of their lives. Dad was elated!

Fathers, let's take seriously the command to train our children. When we ask God for wisdom and rely on the Holy Spirit to direct us, we can trust God to work in our children's lives for their good.

Week 74

A Little Chocolate

THE TANKER TRUCK PULLED out of the Ocean Spray Cranberries parking lot in Markham, WA, and headed to Los Angeles. When it arrived there, the 3500 gallons of cranberry syrup would be processed into a liqueur for one of the airline companies and at $25/ gallon (1978 prices) it was an important order for Ocean Spray.

Two days later the liqueur company called our plant. "Something's wrong with the cranberry syrup," they complained, and then added, "It smells tainted."

An inspector analyzed the syrup and isolated the funny smell, which was chocolate milk. Evidently, the truck driver hadn't cleaned his tanks from his previous delivery well enough and the leftover chocolate residue ruined our shipment of cranberry syrup.

There was no recourse. Instead of the airport, the $90,000 worth of cranberry syrup ended up at a Los Angeles dump and the trucking company learned an expensive lesson about the value of cleanliness.

Obviously, cleanliness is important in food processing. Not only must the food be clean, but the containers that it is stored and shipped in must be also. If the container is contaminated, so is the product and it then becomes unusable for its intended purposes.

You and I were created to be vessels, or containers, for the living God. When we put our faith in Jesus Christ, He comes and lives inside us. Ephesians 3:22 tells us, "And in Him you too are being built together to become a dwelling in which God lives by His Spirit." With this in mind, we can understand how important it is for us to be clean vessels that are free from the contamination of sin.

Just like a little chocolate syrup in our cranberry syrup ruined the whole shipment, so a little sin in our lives can ruin the blessings that God wants to produce in us and through us. Just as *"A little leaven works through the whole batch of dough"* (Gal. 5:9), so a little sin works through our whole lives.

If you discover that there is even a little sin in your life, don't be content to leave it there. We can take that sin to Jesus Christ, confessing it to Him, believing that *"He is faithful and just to forgive us our sins, and to cleanse us from all unrighteousness."* (1 John 1:9)

When we do this with a sincere heart, Christ not only forgives our sin, but He makes us clean and usable for His purposes in our lives. 2 Timothy 2:21 promises, *"If a man cleanses himself from the later, he will be an instrument for noble purposes, made holy, useful to the Master and prepared to do any good work."*

Don't take a chance on ruining the whole "cargo". Let Jesus Christ cleanse you of all your sins, even the so-called little ones. It feels good to be clean and useful for the Master.

Week 75

Driver's Ed

A DRIVER'S EDUCATION student lacked the necessary skills she needed to pass her driver's test, and she was in danger of flunking her class. Her instructor, who cared about her, offered to give her a special session on a little used gravel road behind town, if she was willing to meet him on Saturday morning.

They met early the next Saturday morning and she listened as her instructor gave directions. They started down the gravel road until she came to a large pothole that stretched across the road. Unsure what to do, she stopped the car and looked at her instructor with a questioning look.

Seeing indecision, he explained, "There's room to drive between the pothole and the bank on the right." Then he added, "Go slow and you'll make it okay."

Steering to the right, the girl drove up onto the steep side bank until the car threatened to roll over. Alarmed, she stopped and looked at her instructor with fear.

Hanging by the armrest, the instructor looked down at the scared student and calmly asked, "Is this where you want to be?"

"No," she answered meekly as she studied their precarious situation.

"Do you think you should go frontwards or backwards?" he calmly asked her.

"Backwards?" she guessed.

"Backup, then," he suggested. "We'll try again."

Back to their starting position, she put the car in forward and drove up on the side bank again. Unflustered, the instructor held onto the armrest and repeated his question, "Is this where you want to be?"

"No," she shook her head.

"Should you go frontwards or backwards?", he repeated.

"Backwards," she answered more confidently.

Finally, backing up, the girl put the car in drive and plowed through the pothole! It wasn't pretty, but she made it to the other side.

The point is, despite two failures, the student driver eventually drove past the pothole in the road. The instructor could have chewed her out for her failures, but that would have discouraged her. He could have told her, "Get out. I'm driving now", but that might have embittered her. Instead, he remembered his goal of helping this girl become a safe and mature driver. His ultimate purpose was to put her in a position where she could succeed at driving. Because he was patient with her, this girl eventually earned her driver's license and was able to travel safely wherever she needed to go.

I'm so thankful we have a patient God! If we are willing, He works with us until we pass the course, whatever it may be. Often, we feel ignorant, slow, and unresponsive. Still, if we come to God willingly and with faith, He never loses His patience with us.

Peter tells us, *"He is patient with you, not wanting any to perish, but everyone to come to repentance."* (2 Peter 3:9) If you've heard God's call in your life, don't worry about your failures or lack of ability, but depend on the God who is able to do more than we can comprehend. You too, can learn life's lessons and pass the course that God has laid out for you, if you will only listen to Him and obey His instructions. Nothing is impossible with God!

About the Author

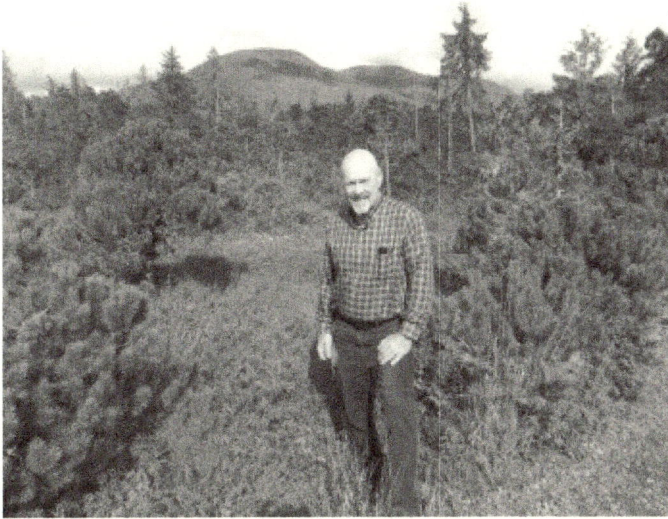

PASTOR JIM RICHARDS grew up in Shelton, WA, self-proclaimed Christmas Tree capital of the world. He served in the Air Force during the Vietnam War and then graduated from Pacific Lutheran University, where he played football, with a BA in Economics. He met and married Janella Teppo at PLU. They were married 32 wonderful years and had four children (3 sons, 1 daughter). Janella died of breast cancer after fighting the disease for 16 years.

He and Sondra Sweet were married in 2006. Together, they have 18 grandchildren. Jim's oldest son Justin died of cancer in 2013. Jim worked in the food processing industry before resigning from Ocean Spray Cranberries in 1979 and attending Multnomah Bible College in Portland, OR. He joined Village Missions in 1980 and pastored small, rural churches in Idaho, Montana and Eastern Washington for 12 years.

In 1980, Pastor Newt Rasor asked Jim to return to his home church, Copalis Community Church, in Copalis Beach, WA, and assume leadership there. As of 2021 he has served there 29 years and is the second pastor in the 88 years since Copalis Community Church began in 1933. Jim's weekly TV program *Raise the Tide* can be seen on christiancableministries.com at 3 pm Monday; 7:30 pm Thursday; 10 am Friday; and 11:00 am Sunday (PST). Jim's third son Jeremy and his wife Stacy (and their 10 children) assist him in the ministry in Copalis Beach.

Jim thanks God for the many Christian brothers and sisters who attend the church in Copalis Beach. He also remembers and thanks God for the saints who have gone on to glory or greener pastures. He gives special thanks to his wife Sondra who is a wonderful helper in his ministry. He devotes this devotional book to his children and grandchildren, praying that they will follow him in his faith, believing that God rewards those who are committed to worshipping and serving Jesus Christ.

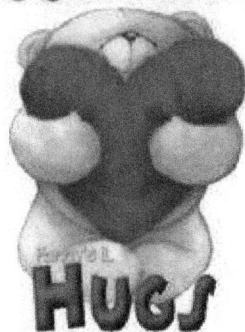

Reviews are hugs
for authors.
Hug your authors!

HUGS

If you like this book, be sure to leave a review.

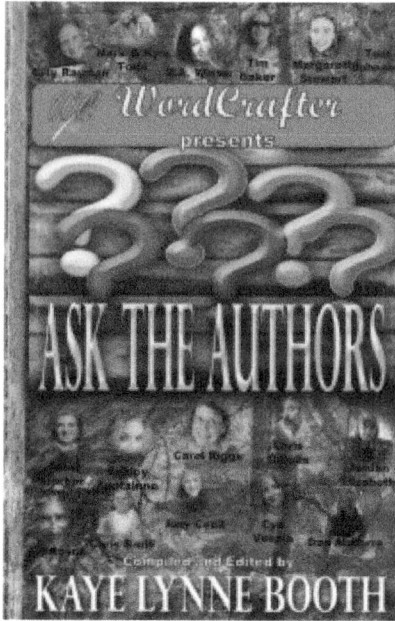

Visit the *WordCrafter* website and social media pages:
Website: https://kayebooth.wixsite.com/wordcrafter
Facebook: https://www.facebook.com/WordCrafterServices/
LinkedIn: https://www.linkedin.com/company/
wordcrafter-enterprises/?viewAsMember=true

Made in the USA
Las Vegas, NV
26 January 2021